TOO IMPORTANT
TO FAIL

Also by Tavis Smiley

Books

Fail Up: *20 Lessons on Building Success from Failure*

What I Know for Sure: *My Story of Growing Up in America*

Covenant with Black America
—Edited by Tavis Smiley

THE COVENANT In Action
—Compiled by Tavis Smiley

Doing What's Right: *How to Fight for What You Believe—and Make a Difference*

Keeping the Faith

Hard Left

How to Make Black America Better
—Edited by Tavis Smiley

DVDs/CDs

STAND: *a film by Tavis Smiley*

On Air: *The Best of Tavis Smiley on the Tom Joyner Morning Show 2004–2008 4-CD commemorative set with booklet*

◈ ◆ ◈

Please visit the distributor of SmileyBooks: Hay House USA: **www.hayhouse.com®**; Hay House Australia: **www.hayhouse.com.au**; Hay House UK: **www.hayhouse.co.uk**; Hay House South Africa: **www.hayhouse.co.za**; Hay House India: **www.hayhouse.co.in**

TOO IMPORTANT TO FAIL

SAVING AMERICA'S BOYS

TAVIS SMILEY REPORTS

SMILEYBOOKS

Distributed by Hay House, Inc.
Carlsbad, California • New York City
London • Sydney • Johannesburg
Vancouver • Hong Kong • New Delhi

Library of Congress Control Number: 2011915809

Tradepaper ISBN: 978-1-4019-3911-3
Digital ISBN: 978-1-4019-3912-0

14 13 12 11   4 3 2 1
1st edition, September 2011
Printed in the United States of America

"It is easier to build strong children than to repair broken men."

—*Frederick Douglass*

Contents

FOREWORD
BY TAVIS SMILEY

Too Important to Fail was produced with funding from the Corporation for Public Broadcasting, as part of its American Graduate: Let's Make It Happen initiative, launched in May 2011 to combat the high school dropout epidemic in the United States. Public radio and television stations have committed to engage their communities and together to determine how best to tackle the American educational crisis.

As the American Graduate initiative has confirmed:

Every year, approximately 1.3 million students drop out of high school—that's 7,000 students a day. On average, only 72 percent of America's children graduate. Less than 60 percent of Latino, African American, and Native American students earn a high school diploma. For minority males, the number has been consistently near or below the 50 percent mark.

The economic impact of children dropping out of high school amounts, over their lifetimes, to a third of a trillion dollars in lost wages, productivity, and taxes. The median earnings for individuals who do not complete high school are $12,000 a year. Those who receive a high school diploma earn, on average, an additional $10,000 a year. According to children who have already left school and those who are at risk for doing so, dropping out establishes almost an insurmountable obstacle in their lives, depriving them of both opportunity and hope.

This is an American tragedy. But it is a tragedy we can correct.

This project has personal meaning for me. Having been blessed to have lived through many of the challenges facing Black boys today, I became consumed with the idea of exploring the institutional benefits and deficiencies, the human and societal contributions or lack thereof that determine promising outcomes for some, and tragic endings for far too many of America's disadvantaged children.

The challenges facing the public school system and the education of all our children are just too vast to address adequately within a one-hour television special. For example, we were not able to fully dissect the conflicting opinions that seem to bar us from an excellent education for all—such as political posturing and finagling against the backdrop of an upcoming election year, union resistance, teacher demoralization, the charter school versus public school debate, or state budgetary crises. With this special, the fifth in the TAVIS SMILEY REPORTS series, we unapologetically examined the crisis that Black boys in America's schools face, and we challenged our viewers to examine their roles in addressing this educational catastrophe.

We traveled to Chicago, Philadelphia, Oakland, and Los Angeles to meet boys who stand at the crossroads and those who are on the road to success. We explored promising, innovative programs and approaches that can make a difference in public schools or charter schools, and we met some of the dedicated educators who refuse to let these Black boys fail.

Sadly, however, the people we met and the approaches we observed, which seem to be working in some of these communities, are not established enough to reverse a nationwide calamity. Every day, thousands of Black boys drop out of school, with far too many headed to our nation's juvenile detention centers and adult prisons.

What's driving this crisis? Overcrowding, underfunded schools, poverty, lack of positive male role models, inattentive adults, misguided policies and poorly conceived mandates, and economic stagnation. Yes, these factors contribute to the problem. It's also about race in America and the cultural differences inherent in our complicated history. It's a problem that cannot be solved without taking an honest and clear-eyed look at how race factors into the reality of lost young lives in a land of promise and opportunity.

This companion book was developed to extend the conversation we started in the special report. Our desire here is to support those who are committed to restoring Black males' confidence in education and reducing dropout rates while increasing college enrollment rates, whether they be parents, teachers, mentors, policy makers, or community leaders. In the back of this book you will find a wealth of information, including educational, institutional, and grassroots resources and strategies; studies and relevant research material; recommended reading lists; and links to engaged and involved organizations, some very likely in your area.

I invite you to explore this material often. Make sure it's always accessible. It is a resource tool to help communities, groups, and individuals—collectively and personally—employ strategies that will help our children succeed.

Too Important to Fail exposed only a sliver of a massive American problem. Yet within that shard, I believe, we went beyond sensational headlines and biased stereotypes and humanized the crisis. You saw the faces of real boys where they live and grow: on a basketball court, in school hallways and classrooms, on perilous streets, and, unfortunately, in juvenile detention centers. You listened to their stories and testimonies, witnessed some of their trials and tribulations, and, I maintain, heard their oh-so-subtle pleas for somebody, anybody, to care enough to stem the bleeding, to end the crisis.

What will it take to end the crisis? No one has all the answers.

What we have done is thrown down the gauntlet and, hopefully, inspired you to explore this most urgent challenge. We have shown you just a few of the faces of those impacted by—and those trying to deal with—the multilayered, complicated forces. We urge you to remember those faces as we seek solutions. Now is the time for us to steady our resolve and for all of us to join together to confront this crisis with a unified battle cry: These boys, America's Black boys, are *too important to fail*!

Tavis Smiley
September 2011
Los Angeles, CA

CHAPTER 1

A

BY ANY OTHER NAME

If a boy born in 2001—no matter his race, creed, or color—has a one-in-three chance of going to prison sometime in his lifetime, shouldn't that be a cause for collective concern? If 85 percent of these kids do not read or do math at grade level in the fourth grade, and if more than half of these boys drop out of high school each and every year, wouldn't that qualify as a national crisis?

Yes, definitely, of course . . . if those boys were white. That, at least, is the opinion of many who are working in the trenches to curtail an undeclared catastrophe in our nation's schools. In reality, those depressing facts and figures apply to Black boys in America. If the scenario shifted and the same tragic statistics affected young white males, educational experts say Americans' mostly lackadaisical response would be a whole lot different.

"It would be immediate. It would be dramatic," argues noted Chicago educator, author, and counselor Dr. Jawanza Kunjufu. "For example, if 53 percent were the dropout rate for white males, it would be unacceptable; if 41 percent of their children were being placed in special education, that would be a major crisis. If only 20 percent of their boys were proficient in reading in eighth grade, that would be a crisis. If only 2.5 percent of white males ever earned a college degree, that would be a major crisis in America."

Every year, 1.3 million American students, roughly 7,000 a day, drop out of America's high schools. Increasingly, more students are dropping out *before* entering high school. As bad as this is for all kids, failure falls on the shoulders of African American boys, who are disproportionately ensnared in the penal system after leaving school. Public education, once the great leveler, is failing these boys at rates that, by any measure, have reached crisis proportions.

In an interview with the *Amsterdam News*, Phillip Jackson, the executive director of the Chicago-based Black Star Project, a nonprofit committed to eliminating the racial academic achievement gap, offered a depressing analysis: "America has lost a generation of Black boys. It is too late. In education, employment economics, incarceration, health, housing, and parenting, we have lost a generation of young Black men," Jackson said before posing the uncomfortable question himself: "Will we lose the next two or three generations, or possibly every generation of Black boys hereafter to negative media, gangs, drugs, poor education, unemployment, father absence, crime, violence, and death?"

The numbers are clear, yet the crisis remains largely unnamed. Why? Is it because the problem is too overwhelming, too entrenched, too institutionalized? Could it be that the criminal actions of some of these dismissed young boys blight our collective compassion? Do most Americans have trouble attaching emotions, feelings, and faces to this calamity?

Brandon, age 16, a junior, and Jamill, age 17, a senior, are but two of those faces. A few years ago, these Philadelphia youths were on their way to becoming just two more statistics, boys prepared to surrender their life chances before getting to know their life choices. Both come from low-income, high-crime neighborhoods. Both were poor achievers in elementary school and were disruptive in classes. Brandon and Jamill were assigned to Daniel Boone, an alternative disciplinary school for misbehaving youth. At Boone the boys stayed in trouble, and neither saw a promising future at the school.

"I'd say what was keeping me in trouble was basically my friends, like who I chose to hang out with," Brandon explained. "That's when I started messing up real bad. I just felt like I was gonna sell drugs, like I could just drop out, I would never come back."

The disciplinary school, Jamill said, displayed no interest in his success or failure: "They didn't really care too much about your grades; they just wanted you to behave."

Jamill had no intention of staying at a school that he felt would forever mark him as a troublemaker: "I wasn't trying to graduate from there. I mean, to graduate and my college application say 'Daniel Boone' . . . It's like, you know, once people heard I was at Daniel Boone, it's like, 'He's a bad kid.'"

Today, it seems Jamill and Brandon have a better chance at beating the massive odds stacked against them. Since leaving middle school, they are thriving at Promise Academy at Roberts Vaux High School. The high school, in North Philadelphia, is 1 of 6 public schools, out of the district's 265, that operate under the Promise Academy model. Teachers are paid slightly more than the national average at the schools. The academies take a holistic approach to educating young people, offering extended school days, Saturday classes, innovative extracurricular activities, and an intense focus on reading, math, and learning a second language.

Neither Jamill nor Brandon thought he would like Roberts Vaux. They'd heard the school enforces a strict dress code. Boys have to wear crisp blue blazers, tan khakis, and a tie. Before attending Roberts Vaux, Jamill had worn a tie only once, to a wedding.

In addition to a dress code, the boys were gifted with something else they hadn't received in elementary or middle school—a positive, Black male influence in the form of William C. Wade, the former principal at Roberts Vaux. (Wade was named principal of Philadelphia's Martin Luther King High School, a new Promise Academy, in June 2011.)

Having a one-on-one relationship with an educator, who was committed to the development of his students, meant a lot to Brandon: "Being as though I don't have my father in my life . . . somebody I can really look up to . . . that's a big thing for me. I can just go to him and talk about anything. And if I ever need something, anything, I can go to Mr. Wade."

What's taken for granted at many schools with a majority of white students is an important missing ingredient in schools charged with reaching and teaching Black boys who have neither a father nor a positive adult male role model in the home. An African American boy can go from preschool to sixth grade without ever coming in contact with an African American male teacher.

In his speeches and writings, Dr. Jawanza Kunjufu notes that 83 percent of America's teachers are white and female. Since the *Brown vs. Topeka Board of Education* case in 1954, there has been a 66 percent decline in African American teachers. Presently, Kunjufu stresses, only 7 percent of American teachers are African American, while the student body is 17 percent African American. African American males, he adds, account for only 1 percent of the teaching force, and the majority are employed in junior and senior high schools.

Although Kunjufu desires to see more Black male teachers in public schools, particularly teaching the earlier grades, he's equally concerned about other contributing factors like teachers who can't teach and the union's influence in the public school system.

"My argument is not against the governing side (of unions), but more about the advocacy and representation given to ineffective teachers," Kunjufu explains. "Many educators are not comfortable challenging unions." Former Federal Secretary of Education Roderick Paige has documented this in his research. Paige explains how it takes almost $100,000 for school systems to legally fight to achieve their objective of removing an ineffective teacher.

Apparently, disproportionate numbers of "ineffective" and unqualified teachers are assigned to low-income schools. According to the 2010 report, *Not Prepared for Class: High-Poverty Schools Continue to Have Fewer In-Field Teachers*, published by the Education Trust, students in low-income communities are disproportionately taught by unqualified teachers. The research shows that "out-of-field" (educators who teach subjects they have not been certified in or majored in college) teach "core classes" at high-poverty secondary schools at a rate of approximately 21.9 percent, compared to 10.9 percent in schools with low poverty levels. In addition, the report states that one in every four secondary math classes in high-poverty schools is taught by a teacher with neither a math major nor certification in math.

"This puts low-income students at a huge disadvantage, both in terms of achievement in math and overall school success," researchers said, noting that success in math is a predictor of future success.

In May 2011, U.S. Education Secretary Arne Duncan joined Congressman Steny Hoyer (D-MD), and other leaders and educators at Bowie State University, a historically Black institution, to tout the Education Department's TEACH campaign (www.TEACH.gov), which raises awareness about the teaching profession and encourages more minorities, especially males, to pursue classroom careers.

The Children's Defense Fund's Freedom School effort, funded by the Kauffman Foundation, has made the audacious commitment to train 5,000 teachers to "carry on the struggle for a fair playing field for all children." At least half of these trainees will be Black males, the agency promises, who will be encouraged to fill as many classrooms as possible over the next few years.

Are skin color and gender really that important in the nation's schools? For Brandon, the simple fact that he was able to talk to a Black male figure of authority at the school inspired him to try harder: "I was on the verge of being kicked out of my old school, but I was able to transfer here, and Mr. Wade said, 'I'll make you a deal . . . You come here and you do what you're supposed to do. I'm going let you come here, you just gotta tell me what you're going to do, what you're supposed to do, and not make me look bad.' It was like he was telling me, don't let him down."

Jamill admits that his temper in school got him into a lot of trouble: "When I was in middle school, I just was going off in anger, like if I get mad, or I just do anything, I wouldn't think about suspension or nothing like that."

Tall, with an athletic build and a dark complexion, Jamill fits a profile that many teachers can't understand or cope with, said Principal Wade. "The easiest thing to do is run a young man out of your classroom or run him out of your school. African American males are very intimidating to some people, because the baggage they bring through the front door causes them to act out in classes when they are falling behind academically," Wade explained.

Black boys are "confrontational because they want to be educated," Wade argues. And there are some teachers, he adds, who hold grudges against Black boys who bring their baggage to school. But the true gist of an educator's work, he insists, is figuring out how to get over those hang-ups and find ways to truly improve the learning experience of Black boys. Which, Wade says, he challenges all of the teachers under his charge to do.

In the interview for the PBS special *Too Important to Fail,* Wade described young Black males as "victims." It's a word not often ascribed to the students, but an important one nevertheless.

"Black boys are impacted by several things that plague urban areas," Wade said. They reside in high-crime areas, witness undesirable events both in the home and outside of it, and live in single-parent homes because fathers or mothers are incarcerated. They suffer from things that they should not be exposed to, and don't have control over. So, they're unwilling casualties of society's ills because they didn't write it this way.

If the crisis is to be averted, Wade said, educators must recognize Black boys as victims of society and develop creative ways to remove obstacles.

Losing Promise

Many in Philadelphia consider Dr. Arlene Ackerman a maverick in education. The former superintendent of schools lobbied hard for extra money—$7.2 million more for the 2011–12 school years alone—to operate the Promise Academy schools. This was at a time when the district had to cut more than $600 million from its budget.

Ackerman, who stepped down from her position in August 2011, had her share of budgetary battles, union fights and controversy with politicians and Philadelphia's School Reform Commission. She's taken hits for replacing long-tenured teachers at the academies with some educators fresh out of college. Ackerman says she wanted the "best and the brightest" teachers who are fully committed to working with underserved populations—even if they are fresh out of college. She bumped heads with union and district officials when she shielded 174 Promise Academy teachers from the district's mandatory 1,200 teacher lay-off to satisfy its huge budget deficit. The layoffs would have destabilized the model she was trying to create with the Promise Academies, Ackerman insisted.

School Reform Commission Chairperson Robert Archie praised Ackerman's accomplishments in just three years: "Dr. Ackerman demonstrated real results: three years of gains in test scores; a 29 percent decline in violent incidents; 7 percent gains in the six-year graduation rates; and lastly, Parent University where more than 40,000 parents took courses throughout the past three years."

Ackerman's short tenure with the Philadelphia Public School District takes us to a disturbing place. Keep in mind: there are only six Promise Academies (two high schools, one middle school, and three elementary schools) out of the 265 schools in the district. In essence, they are charter schools within the public school structure. No one knows what effect Ackerman's departure will have on the effort. Although its preliminary success has been noted, the experimental effort comes at a huge price, one that—in this economy—most public schools can't afford.

On the battlefield of school reform, it seems good intentions aren't enough. While grownups wage wars about budgets, tenure, and political influence, low-income kids are caught in the crossfire with targets especially affixed on the backs of Black boys. If public schools are failing our kids, why not pull the plug on public schools?

CHARTER A NEW COURSE?

The Obama Administration are big fans of charter schools. The President has called for the expansion of the number of charter schools and suggested replicating those that seem to be working.

Most charter schools are publicly funded and accountable for public tax dollars. Unlike public schools, charters do not operate under the traditional Board of Education structure. Charters make legislative contracts or "charters" with the state which exempt them from certain state and local rules and regulations. Charter school staffers are not bound by union contracts. The schools are reviewed every 3 years or so and charters can be revoked if they don't comply with their approved standards. So, conversely, charters can be more experimental and innovative.

Why not just dump the old system and create a nation of charter schools? There are a couple of good reasons why that will never happen. The first relates to numbers. According to the U.S. Department of Education, National Center for Education Statistics about 1.4 million students attend the almost 5,000 charter schools in the country. On the other hand, about 50 million children attend public schools.

As the Philadelphia experiment illustrates, it costs big money to create and operate quality charter schools. Public school systems employ about 3.3 million teachers. The government cannot afford to create a new educational system nor can politicians, particularly on the Left, afford to alienate more than 3 million voters.

Critics bemoan the fact that charter schools can choose the cream of the crop. Public schools have to take every child no matter the environment from which they come. Although most use a lottery system, charters can pick and choose their students. They can choose to accept high-achievers and more well-behaved children, which leaves the low-achievers and the more unmanageable kids for public schools. An all-out movement to expand charter schools under the current scenario would extract money already needed in underfunded public schools.

Another concern is that charters are no better than public schools. A 2010 multi-state study by Mathematica Policy Research showed that, on average, kids who attend charter schools did no better than their peers at public schools. In 2009, the Center for Research on Education Outcomes (CREDO) found no market difference between kids who attended public schools and charter schools.

It must be noted however, that charter schools operating under the KIPP (Knowledge Is Power Program) umbrella showed positive outcomes. Also, the Mathematica study did find "nuanced evidence" that the most effective charter schools are the ones serving lower-income students, especially in urban areas.

With these facts in mind, the charter/public school hybrid may be the most cost-effective means to conduct the experiments. Public schools have an established structure. We cannot allow the foundation to crumble while investing in experiments. Administrators like Geoffrey Canada with New York's Harlem Children's Zone, Ackerman and other innovators believe they are discovering the essential elements that can help low-income students excel in public or charter schools. If these fundamentals can be applied in either public or charter school settings, they believe the country can start to turn the tide that's left so many youth, especially Black boys, awash upon the shores of hopelessness.

THE PRECONDITIONS TO LEARNING

In order to make Promise Academies live up to their promise, Dr. Arlene Ackerman insisted that her schools must be equipped to deal with the preconditions of learning. Each school has a cadre of mentors, counselors, behavioral specialists, student advisers, and conflict-resolution managers to help address the personal, family, and societal wounds inflicted upon the students.

"What we did was put social workers in those schools to connect the families to social services. We put extra teachers in those schools, counselors, and nurses—all of the conditions that we know have to be in place so that young people can learn, we put in place."

Unfortunately, Ackerman says, schools are expected to deal with conditions that haven't been figured out in the larger society or that Americans refuse or "don't have the will" to deal with.

"Things like health care for young people, homelessness and young people, a variety of issues. Violence that often, you know, is in the neighborhood," Ackerman explained, adding "and before you can expect young people to learn, to pay attention, you have to address those other kinds of issues.

"In Philadelphia we've found that when we address those issues, these young people show dramatic improvement, and it doesn't take a long time. But there are certain preconditions for learning that must take place. Young people have to come to school ready to learn, so I think it's really important that we take a look at all those preconditions for learning and make sure they're in place and then our children can learn," Ackerman said.

President Barack Obama's Promise Neighborhoods initiative is an expansion of Geoffrey Canada's Harlem Children's Zone in New York. Theoretically, the idea is to create areas, or zones, in disadvantaged areas where children are provided everything they need—academically, medically, and socially—to succeed and achieve throughout their school years.

The Black Community Crusade for Children, a Children's Defense Fund campaign, is committed to replicating the Harlem Children's Zone model in other communities through President Obama's Promise Neighborhoods initiative so all children, especially Black boys, can navigate the dysfunction that has infiltrated many low-income communities.

PARENTS AS PARTNERS

Brandon lives with his two sisters, a cousin, his mother, and his severely handicapped 11-year-old brother. The blocks surrounding his home are testimonials to the odd dichotomy that constitutes his environment. Rich, resilient African American culture is sullied with profanity-spewing youngsters in bass-booming cars. Drab, vacant buildings stand right across the street or adjacent to buildings covered entirely with murals that tell the Philly story in vibrant blues, oranges, yellows, and reds. For the TV special, Brandon leans against the wall of one of those brilliantly painted buildings. Animated birds soar in blue skies as Brandon describes how his younger brother, who has Down syndrome, occupies most of his mother's time. "There's a lot of responsibility, like . . . all her attention [can't] be on me because she gotta take care of my little brother, so it's kinda hard. My little brother, he got to always go to doctors' appointments, like surgeries and all kinds of stuff, so it's a lot of pressure. That's why I try to stay out of the way and do, like, the best I can . . . just do everything right," Brandon said.

Ackerman said she and the personnel at all of the Promise Academy schools are also trying to do "everything right" to help parents who are dealing with the same social and economic dysfunctions that impact their children.

When filming the PBS special, cameras captured a glass-encased sign on the lawn of Roberts Vaux High School. PARENTS ARE OUR PARTNERS, it read.

The words are more than a feel-good slogan, Ackerman insists: "Parental engagement is key. It's incumbent upon the school system to engage parents in a way that . . . we come to where they are, instead of expecting them to come to where we are."

A School Advisory Council of parents and community members helps make decisions at the schools. Ackerman instituted "Parent University" at Promise Academies, where adults take parenting courses and learn of other ways to address their children's needs at home. To date, 22,000 parents, many of them parents of African American boys, according to Ackerman, have been involved with the schools or have taken Parent University classes.

"You can visit any Promise Academy and see parents in the hallways, because we're reaching out. We've found authentic ways to get them involved. That's a priority for us. For many of our young people who have attended schools that have traditionally underperformed, their parents and grandparents went to those schools. Changing a school means changing the community, and engaging the entire community, not just the young people who are attending those schools, but their parents and the larger community as well," Ackerman said.

It's an established fact that without parental involvement, most students will not succeed in school. Public schools across the country are challenged to find ways to get parents engaged with teachers in the educational process.

In St. Louis, Missouri, Karen Kalish, a local philanthropist, created a nonprofit dedicated to reviving the tradition of teachers visiting the homes of the students they teach.

HOME WORKS! The Teacher Home Visit Program (www.teacherhomevisit.org) makes arrangements and provides the introductions and transportation so teachers and other educators can visit their students' homes. Through the program, teachers gain valuable insights into their students' lives and get to know parents personally. Home visits help some parents to feel less intimidated and motivates them to become more involved in their child's education. Mostly, Kalish says, children know that the adults in their lives care about them and want them to succeed.

CONFRONTING THE CRISIS

Jamill is one of nine kids. If he graduates and goes on to college, he says he will be the first Black male in his family to do so. His sister went. His cousin started but didn't finish. That means Jamill will be the first boy in his family—immediate and extended—to graduate from college. The prospect excites him: "My cousin had a chance, but . . . he just stopped. I thought he was gonna do it; he was gonna help me, motivate me more . . . so I'm, like, I got to go now."

Taking Jamill's and Brandon's hopes and aspirations into account, and factoring in the promises and possibilities offered by the Promise Academy schools, the crisis facing Black boys remains unabated and largely ignored. With looming federal budget cuts that will tear holes in the social safety net, with a nation still stymied by race and addicted to the criminal justice system as panacea for uneducated and misunderstood Black boys, nothing is promised.

A serious question remains unanswered: Why should America care about Black boys being left behind?

"Because we're all Americans," Ackerman answers. "We're part of the fabric of this country, and if we have young people who are barely surviving, our country will never thrive. It's beginning to show in our competitiveness in the world. Everybody has to thrive; everybody has to do well. So it's in our best interests—white America, Black America, all of America—that all of our young people achieve and achieve at high levels, if we want to remain number one."

The Alliance for Excellent Education, a national policy and advocacy organization, estimates that every year, more than 1 million students (7,000 kids per school day) will not graduate from high school on time. Of that number, 54 percent are African American students. The organization stresses that America cannot afford to ignore the effect this national dropout rate will have on society.

Alliance for Excellent Education (www.all4ed. org) reinforces Ackerman's point. The national nonprofit organization estimates that if the 1.3 million high school dropouts from the class of 2010 had earned their diplomas, the U.S. economy would have seen an additional $337 billion in wages over these students' lifetimes. Further, it states, "If this annual pattern is allowed to continue, 13 million students will drop out of school during the next decade at a cost to the nation of more than $3 trillion."

The economic indicators of having so many Black boys drop out of high school are alarming but should not be the spark that ignites a country to action. Rosa Smith, former president and CEO of the Schott Foundation for Public Education, said that aggressively addressing the downward trend for Black boys in school and society serves as a litmus test for America's leaders. The former school superintendent encourages school administrators to lead in ways that nurture the "student group most vulnerable to school failure."

Principal Williams agrees with Smith: Saving Black boys is indeed America's litmus test, he said. "We have to stop looking at these boys as if they are expendable."

CHAPTER 2

SURVIVAL SKILLS:

READ

OR DIE

"We are Black brothers united—not thieves or junkies that steal to feed senseless addictions. We are addicts that steal knowledge to feed our minds. We are not dim, senseless fools but intelligent men, beyond measure . . ."

Dr. Alfred W. Tatum paces the classroom, arms crossed, dissecting the words of the student who reads his work aloud. The other boys in the room, about a dozen, are also carefully listening. They know Tatum will have them interpret their classmate's impassioned writings when he's finished.

The young author is 1 of the 15 lucky ones chosen from out of more than 100 Chicago-area applicants who applied for Tatum's African American Adolescent Male Summer Literacy Institute. Tatum, an associate professor at the University of Illinois–Chicago, started the program four years ago. Through reading, writing, and staunch advocacy, Tatum hopes to foster a generation of socially conscious, self-reliant thinkers unafraid to embrace their Black identity. Scholastic, the world's largest publisher and distributor of children's books, supports the professor's initiative, which meets for 15 days in the summer at the University of Illinois–Chicago.

Tatum uses a variety of fiction and nonfiction texts as tools to encourage Black adolescent males to communicate the multiple, complex contexts that shape their lives. Tatum has written more than 50 articles and authored two award-winning books on literacy development and teaching Black boys the lifesaving rewards of reading and writing.

"Lifesaving" is no understatement. According to the 2010 National Assessment of Educational Progress report, four out of five fourth graders from low-income families are not proficient in reading. The Children's Defense Fund reports that 85 percent of Black children do not read or do math at grade level by the fourth grade. In other words, if these children have not become proficient readers by the third grade, more than likely they will give up or drop out of high school, which almost guarantees another generation of Black kids with educational failure and poverty cemented into their futures.

"This will occur unless the roles of reading and writing are re-conceptualized in our nation," says Dr. Tatum. "Educators must find ways to score with reading and writing, not simply focus on reading and writing scores. Too few Black boys find reading and writing in schools meaningful. They find that both fail to compete with their out-of-school realities. Sadly, many literacy reform efforts and teaching practices muscle Black boys toward failure because they are not designed to acknowledge or interrupt the comfortable social arrangement of too many Black boys at or near the bottom of the academic food chain."

"We seek higher learning through education and study rather than skill in the fields. We move in the direction of progress not in the direction of idle confusion. And as Black Americans, we accomplish dreams through work and our reality."

Finished, the young man awaits feedback.

"Comments?" Tatum shouts.

The magic begins. Boys, many of whom previously saw no value in school, in books, or in reading, accept Tatum's invitation to use words as conduits for their feelings, frustrations, and analyses of their often chaotic worlds. They use their pens to re-imagine themselves.

"Many of these boys initially write from a space of turmoil, of vulnerabilities, things that they see in their day-to-day existence," Tatum explained during his interview for *Too Important to Fail*. "But quickly they begin to move to broader issues to figure out or make sense of the things that are affecting their lives in their community. They begin to realize that the issues they're wrestling with are issues we're all wrestling with—they just provide a very different lens that oftentimes is ignored in many educational spaces."

Although Tatum's program has received national praise, some experts fear efforts such as his are "too little, too late" for impoverished kids who attend low-performing and under-resourced schools.

"When kids are not reading by fourth grade, they almost certainly get on a glide path to poverty," said Ralph Smith, senior vice president of the Annie E. Casey Foundation and managing director of the Campaign for Grade Level Reading.

Nationally, two out of every three fourth graders are not proficient in reading. The more dismal statistics attached to low-income Black and Latino youth has served as a wake-up call to several organizations dedicated to improving the nation's educational outcomes.

In 2010, the Annie E. Casey Foundation released its KIDS COUNT Special Report, "Early Warning! Why Reading by the End of Third Grade Matters," to raise awareness and spark nationwide action. The effort is supported by a broad coalition of agencies, including America's Promise Alliance, Mission: Readiness, and United Way Worldwide.

Black boys, in particular, represent the bottom tier of students failing to read proficiently at early ages. The NAEP report also found that only 12 percent of Black fourth-grade boys are proficient in reading, compared to 38 percent of white boys.

Although he doesn't dispute the numbers, Tatum takes exception to "too little, too late" assumptions from government and education officials who insist Black boys are lost if they can't read by third grade.

"They have to stop looking at these boys as if they are scorecards of achievement." W. E. B. Du Bois said a long time ago, don't view these boys as scorecards of achievement; recognize their humanity, because parents do not give birth to scorecards of achievement.

"I think the government has to move away from social and structural experimentation that has had unintended consequences for Black boys," Tatum said.

There are no academic requirements to join Tatum's institute. The only requirement is that the boys be willing to write. Sometimes, as he sifts through samples students have submitted for consideration, something "that sings" catches his eye, Tatum says. He has also read submissions with signs of trouble that have urged him to recruit a boy just to hear his story. There was no scorecard for the child he selected a few years ago who ended his submission with the words: "I want to do the suicidal."

"A life was worth living," Tatum said.

The professor worries that statistical data stigmatizes Black boys as inefficient readers and dampens educators' desire to invest in intellectually demanding approaches that reach Black boys after targeted grade levels.

"I think one of the most important things is that we don't become overly concerned that a kid struggles in third and fourth grade, and write them off," Tatum explained. "Their struggles in third and fourth grade become their identity. So we have to juxtapose two things; if a kid is vulnerable, how do I think about instruction and ways to nurture their resilience? And as an educator I have to accept culpability."

Facts Are Facts

Considering that so many Black boys enter high school grossly unprepared, it's imperative to develop, expand, and duplicate solid reading alternatives such as Tatum's Summer Literacy Institute for teens. Still, facts are facts. We can ill afford to dismiss the ramifications of low-income students who miss the milestone. The cost to communities, the country, and lives is too heavy to take lightly.

McKinsey & Company, a global management consulting firm, estimates that if U.S. students had met the educational achievement level of higher-performing nations between 1983 and 1998, the U.S. GDP in 2008 could have been $1.3 trillion to $2.3 trillion higher.

The nation's defenses are weakened by the pool of high school graduates who aren't skilled enough to meet its security needs. The Defense Department estimates that more than 75 percent of Americans aged 17 to 24 are ineligible to join the U.S. military because they are poorly educated, involved in crime, or physically unfit. Even with a high school diploma, 30 percent of potential recruits fail the entrance exam due to inadequate math and reading skills.

"We must get today's kids on track to become tomorrow's leaders," said retired brigadier general Velma Richardson of Missouri, who spoke in favor of the Casey Foundation's KIDS COUNT Special Report.

For its part, the federal government offers grants for early childhood centers aimed at helping ensure that all children enter kindergarten with the necessary language, cognitive, and early-reading skills for continued success in schools.

The Early Reading First initiative was designed to help centers such as Head Start develop stronger reading foundations for preschool-age children. Grants can be used to improve or expand exceptional programs, procure data-based materials, develop sound strategies and curricula, and promote parental engagement and other efforts that may enhance the early reading skills of preschool-age children.

Noting the success of the Harlem Children's Zone, the Obama administration awarded 20 grants in 2010 to cities with plans to replicate the highly praised New York City antipoverty experiment. The Zone follows children from birth to adulthood, providing free and comprehensive educational, social, and medical services for more than 10,000 kids living in the 96 blocks of central Harlem.

One of the Zone's major components is its Baby College, which educates parents about raising children, making sure they understand how their child's brain develops and know what's needed at certain stages to help children succeed in school. Kids enter Harlem Gems, an all-day kindergarten-prep program, at age four; classes are in session from 8 A.M. to 6 P.M. With a four-to-one student-to-teacher ratio, children are taught three languages—French, Spanish, and English—and are provided with comprehensive language, cognitive, and reading lessons.

Geoffrey Canada, founder of the Harlem Children's Zone, rightfully boasts that 100 percent of the students who've attended Baby

College have entered kindergarten at grade level. He takes further pride in the fact that, since starting his program in the 1990s, he's helped to bring up a generation of children with more than 650 attending college today.

Even though Canada has taken steps to help children enter the fourth grade with appropriate grade-level reading and math skills, he's not a big fan of labels or guidelines that determine when a child has passed the cut-off mark for salvation. Canada shared his concerns during a speech in 2008 to Amherst College students: "They keep forcing us to make a decision. 'C'mon, Geoff, you can't do everything. You've got to make a decision. Be tough. Decide. Is it early childhood? Is it middle school?

"You know [when] the most important time in a child's life is?" Canada asked the crowd, before answering. "Today. Right now!"

Although he stresses that there is no expiration date on helping Black boys, Canada absolutely supports sound efforts that encourage kids to read at an early age. However, he too has little patience for tests and data that stigmatize Black boys without leading to conclusive redress.

"I've become clairvoyant about this testing stuff . . . I see in the last five years 76 percent of your kids failed ELA (English Language Arts); this year it will be somewhere between 72 and 78 percent . . . You don't have to be a genius to figure out that doesn't make any sense. But you know what?" Canada continued, "because these kids are poor, nobody cares. They just simply don't care. You just accept failure, and you say, 'tough.'

"We have to change that."

"WE BELIEVE!"

The boys line up row after row, military style, in the school's gymnasium. Each wears a dark, crisp blazer and a red tie. A red and gold crest with back-to-back screaming lions is stamped on the jacket's chest. Shoulders back, heads erect, the boys chant the school's motto:

"We believe in ourselves. We believe in each other. We believe in our prep. WE BELIEVE!" they shout in unison.

Welcome to Urban Prep Academies, a non-profit organization that operates a network of public all-male college-preparatory high schools in Chicago. Urban Prep has been the subject of several national and international news features and programs. The organization became the focus of recent media attention when it was announced in 2010 that 100 percent of its seniors in the schools' first graduating class had been admitted to a four-year college or university.

In Chicago, Urban Prep has debunked the notion that Black boys cannot learn to succeed at high rates. Dr. Jawanza Kunjufu, who serves as a consultant with Urban Prep, said the school's dedication to the success of Black boys is "more than a job, it's almost like a ministry."

"They have a principal who is the instructional leader; they have greater time on task; their curriculum is culturally relevant; their pedagogy is congruent with children's learning styles; they've been able to harness negative peer pressure and turn it into cooperative learning," Kunjufu said, adding that Urban Prep's "best practices" actually work.

Jabryce, an Urban Prep senior, is benefiting from those "best practices." His challenges, like many of his schoolmates, are all too familiar. Jabryce arrives at school from a dangerous urban neighborhood; he lives in a single-parent home with no father in the house, and his immediate and family circles lack any other positive Black male role models.

"Before I came to Urban Prep, I attended Bennett Elementary School. Those weren't the best years of my life," Jabryce recalled. "I was always in trouble—not getting good grades; my mom always had to come to the school. When I came to Urban Prep, it changed my life. I made bonds with my teachers; they helped me a lot. I started getting good grades and started becoming a 3.0 student, being on the honor roll."

Most important, Jabryce said, he started to like school.

"Urban Prep changed my life. It really helped me become a more intelligent man, seeing a future, wanting to go to college and becoming successful."

Jabryce's comments underscore one of the more consistent recipes shared with Urban Prep students. Tim King, founder and president of the academies, notes that his boys come from precarious backgrounds and desperately need to believe that they too can have bright futures.

"There are so many reasons why we're seeing Black boys suffering, and it's hard to pinpoint just one. There are issues with a lack of positive role models in their communities; so many of our students come from single-parent households, most often led by women. Another challenge is the economic system in our country. Right now

Black men have the highest unemployment rate. So, we've got all these factors that are adversely impacting this population—crime, violence, and incarceration at incredibly high rates. Any negative point you can think of, and there are Black men, Black young men, and Black boys at the top of those lists."

Instilling a sense of self-awareness and confidence in Urban Prep students is important to King: "We give our kids swords and shields. The sword is kind of like intellect: They can fight any intellectual battle, because they're really smart—they have got the book stuff down. The shield, that's their protection, confidence, self-awareness, and self-possession. These are the things they need in order to protect themselves in a world that's not going to be filled with welcoming committees."

During the 2009 presidential inauguration, CNN newscaster Don Lemon described Urban Prep students, who had traveled to Washington, DC, for the occasion, as "Little Obamas." The moniker has been repeated several times in the media. Such designations aren't necessarily aligned with test scores, King points out. Urban Prep students, he says, are prepared to excel in environments where the majority of Black boys have never entered or have been unprepared to excel.

"Not only do I think they're academically prepared, but I also believe that they are socially and emotionally prepared, which, frankly, in my view, is the most important point," King said. "I mean, you can score whatever on the ACT, be it at the high end or the low end, but if you can't figure out how, when you're on a college campus, to deal with a wider and often whiter, hostile world, if you don't have that self-possession, self-confidence, and self-awareness to be able to function on that college campus, you're not going to be successful."

While conducting his interview for the PBS special, the host, Tavis Smiley, noted that, despite the success of Urban Prep Academies, many people liken it to "a pebble in the water at the moment," an endeavor that, even if replicated, can't possibly save all Black boys.

King responded with the answer he gave to a critic who had referred to Urban Prep as an "itty, bitty school," telling King that it wasn't going make a significant difference.

"You know, I kind of laughed at that, because that person didn't understand the severity of the crisis and how one 'itty, bitty school' really can move the needle," said King, who offered data to back up his rebuttal. "In Chicago, in the public schools, there will be about 10,000 African American male ninth graders starting school in any given year. Only 2.5 percent will end up with college degrees. That's 250 out of 10,000. Urban Prep graduated 100 kids this year. All of them went to college. If only half make it through, we will have added 20 percent to the number of African American boys who started out in Chicago public schools as ninth graders and ended up with four-year college degrees.

"The itty, bitty school is making a huge, huge difference, but it's only making that difference because the crisis is so severe."

SAVING THE CRYING SOULS

"I have heard a lot of voices in my lifetime. After hearing the voice, I would feel sorrow. I kept thinking to myself; 'There's a little girl slowly dying and nobody's helping her.' She cries and cries but no one hears her tears . . ."

Another boy at the African American Adolescent Male Summer Literacy Institute in Chicago uses prose and metaphors to speak to a world that ignores the pain and suffering of the most vulnerable.

Again, Dr. Tatum paces the floor, hand on chin. The words have not lost meaning with the boy's teacher. After all, this child, like so many others Tatum has reached through his program, fits the profile of a "doomed" kid who wasn't reading proficiently by the fourth grade. Tatum has little patience for those who label Black boys outside of historical and social context.

"We have to rescue the significance of teaching these boys and be unapologetic about it and dismiss those issues of cultural amnesia," he says.

"She may act as if nothing's wrong, but I looked in her soul and found the truth . . ."

Tatum says that nothing gives him greater pride than watching his students evolve. There's something about looking in a young man's eyes and seeing a different person as a result of the experience that helps him carry "his load in very, very powerful ways," Tatum said.

During his interview with Smiley, Tatum explained the difference between learning to read and learning to write.

"The challenge with reading in some cases is to give boys access to the text on the outside of them. Writing gives boys access to the text on the inside of them. It liberates them in many ways. There's just no more cover-up. So writing is used as a tool to access their own humanity.

"It changes me. Each time that I sit down with [them], I become enriched. I sleep better at night knowing that I did all that I can do to move these boys to a different place and space . . . It allows me to feel good that I did all that I could do in a particular moment in space."

Tatum is obviously in that "space" as the student finishes his work:

> "I refuse to sit back and watch that little girl die. Now, we must ask ourselves two questions: Are we willing to let humans die? Or, are you going to save these crying souls?"

CHAPTER 3

WHO'S TEACHING BLACK BOYS AND WHAT DO THEY LEARN?

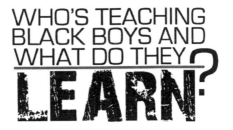

We've seen the Hollywood script dozens of times: A long-suffering, white educator (insert actor of choice: Meryl Streep, Sandra Bullock, Matthew Perry, Michelle Pfeiffer, etc.) is assigned to a ghetto school with dangerous, low-income, smart-ass, and obnoxious "I-just-don't-give-a-damn" students. The benevolent, frustrated, but stubborn teacher refuses to give up on these poor souls. He/she bucks the stale, bureaucratic educational system, to the chagrin of supervisors. He/she helps the deprived students confront their inner-city demons and discover their true gifts, purpose, and worth.

Epilogue: The maligned, mistreated, and misunderstood educator has been vindicated. Pessimistic, frowning, hard-core students have been transformed into smiling, grateful, optimistic vessels of limitless possibilities.

Cue the sentimental music, roll the credits, fade to black.

In real life, there is no fade, just shades of Black—bleak statistics and dismal educational outcomes; Black boys and low-income students failing in schools and languishing in conditions that will lead to gloomy futures; lives punctuated by unemployment, crime, poverty, prison, and early death.

Last year, the Shott Foundation's report *Yes We Can: The 2010 Schott 50 State Report on Black Males in Public Education* showed that the overall 2007–8 graduation rate for Black males in the United States was only 47 percent, and that half of the states experienced graduation rates for Black male students below the national average.

With Black boys perilously high on the "endangered species" list, we must force ourselves to ask the question Tinsel Town tends to gloss over:

Who's teaching these African American boys, and what do they learn?

The hallways of Alameda County Juvenile Justice Center are eerily antiseptic. The eye gravitates to the sparkling diamond-shaped linoleum floor tiles in white, orange, and brown. The tiles provide a much-needed respite from the puke-yellow paint covering the walls and the massive steel doors marked Unit 1, Unit 2, Unit 3, with no ending number in sight.

Against this backdrop, Tavis Smiley spoke with six inmates of the juvenile detention center. Some were "boys" in age only. Already a couple had the demeanor of hardened adult inmates. Others displayed scars on their arms, hands, faces—and in their eyes and on their souls.

Cynicism and the hard look in his eyes seem to fade as Jerrell listened to fellow detainees share their stories or speak of their misdeeds and wounds. Sporting a drab green baseball cap, green jacket, and blue jeans, Jerrell crossed and uncrossed his arms and spoke up when Smiley asked if "trauma" played any role in Black boys winding up in the criminal justice system: "I was, like, in the fourth grade. I had a teacher who told me I wasn't never going to amount to anything, so when I was told that, I was still angry and I just seen a lot of stuff too."

Smiley pressed for elaboration, asking Jerrell if he "bought into that lie."

"No, I didn't buy into it," the young man replied unconvincingly. "It just got to me emotionally. Like for a teacher to tell a student that— you're supposed to embrace your students and make them feel good about themselves. So with that being said, emotionally that hurt."

Emotionally, psychologically, and physically, hundreds of thousands of low-income minority students and an overwhelming number of Black male students are hurt by a system that has yet to acknowledge and honor their personal, educational, or cultural needs. In fact, when statistics are cross-referenced and examined, a spotlight shines on a sinister, institutionalized structure that betrays the promise of opportunity and well-being via a "good education."

Black boys are disproportionately removed from mainstream education by imposing disciplinary interventions or by tracking them into special-education programs, said Dr. Jawanza Kunjufu. Of the Black boys who enter special education, only 10 percent return to the mainstream classroom and stay there and only 27 percent graduate high school. Special education has become metaphorically this century's "door of no return."

"Where have all of our Black sons gone?" asked Dr. Rosa Smith, former president of the Schott Foundation for Public Education, in her December 2003 essay, *Race, Poverty & Special Education: Apprenticeships for Prison Work*. "They are first sent to special-education programs, which for all too many African American boys are not doorways to opportunity, but trapdoors sending them willy-nilly to war, to jail, to lives of unfulfilled promise."

Smith used a snippet from the 2002 President's Commission on Excellence in Special Education report, *A New Era: Revitalizing Special Education for Children and Their Families*, to reinforce her point: "Many of the current methods of identifying children with disabilities lack validity. As a result, thousands of children are misidentified every year . . ."

Prior to passage of the Voting Rights Act in 1965, African Americans in mostly Southern states were denied the right to vote based on their inability to pay the poll tax and their inability to pass rigged literacy tests. Today, Black youth are further disenfranchised through biased standardized tests, critics claim. Smith claims that the reliance on IQ tests with known cultural biases means that "minority children are much more likely to be placed in the emotional disturbance category." Worse yet, these "overclassifications" of African American children as "mentally challenged" are not determined by scientifically trained experts but are overwhelmingly based on teacher referrals. Again quoting from the 2002 special report, Smith wrote, "To the extent that teachers are not prepared to manage behavior or instruct those with learning characteristics that make them 'at risk' in general education, minority children will be more likely to be referred."

Based on the retention, suspension, expulsion, and corporal punishment rates that disproportionately apply to Black children, the Children's Defense Fund indicts America's educational system as a contributor to the devastating Cradle to Prison Pipeline. Data from its Portraits of Inequality study are stunning:

Black children are two and a half times as likely as white children to be held back or retained in school. Although Black students made up only 17 percent of all students in public schools in 2006, they represented:

- 35.6 percent of all students who experienced corporal punishment

- 37.4 percent of all students who were suspended

- 37.9 percent of all students who were expelled

Poor Black children are taught by the least-qualified teachers, who have low expectations of minority students; and they attend the worst educational facilities with the least resources. The "overrepresentation of poor and minority children in grade retention, out-of-school suspensions, and special-education classes" contributes to student discouragement, low self-esteem, and general disengagement from school, the Children's Defense Fund report states.

Black students face "inconsistency in discipline," said Vernon C. Polite, professor at Bowie State University and coeditor of the book *African American Males in School and Society*. Polite conducted his own study and found that for the same offense, suspensions range from 2 days to 22 days. Because federal and state guidelines regarding suspensions and expulsions are fluid and practiced differently state by state, Polite says, large numbers of African American boys wind up meandering through neighborhood streets, some engaging in criminal activity when they'd be better off in schools.

"The very problems we wish to mitigate are being exacerbated," the professor said with obvious frustration.

An African American boy can go from kindergarten to sixth grade without ever coming in contact with an African American male teacher. Dr. Ivory A. Toldson, an associate professor with Howard University's Counseling Psychology program, said the absence of Black male teacher-student contact contributes to some of the "non-academic-related" disparities that impact Black boys, such as placement in special education. He emphasizes the word "nonacademic" because, most of the time, Black boys are placed in special education as a result of their behavior, not their academic capacities.

"A lot of times it's because their behaviors are misunderstood by the staff that works with them. It could also be associated with the disproportionate number of Black males who are suspended," Toldson explained. The research points out that, among Black males, 60 percent of those in school have reported being suspended at least once, compared to about 26 percent of white males who reported their suspensions.

Effectively interacting with Black boys is hampered by teachers of different races, genders, environments, and backgrounds assigned to teach them. Many teachers bring their attitudes about stereotypes and their biases about Black communities and Black children to the classroom.

No doubt, the fourth-grade teacher who told Jerrell he'd never amount to anything in life was probably talking to a stereotype, not to a child who would be emotionally scarred by his words. Imagine the daily indignities schoolchildren in low-income communities face when stopped, searched, and asked their gang affiliation by police. Consider the psychic impact of arriving at school every day, walking through metal detectors, having your backpack searched, and being frisked and treated like a dangerous suspect.

This, Toldson said, is a sign of disrespect that should not be tolerated.

"We have to make sure we are giving Black males [in particular] the basic respect they deserve. When you decide to put up a metal detector at one school but not to do it at another school that's less than ten miles away, because it's a white school, to me, that's a sign of disrespect."

Toldson dismisses claims that these security precautions are necessary at low-income schools. They are more of a psychological benefit than they are effective, he counters. Research, Toldson argues, indicates that the best way to keep weapons away from schools is by cultivating the types of environments where kids willingly tell on other kids who have weapons.

"To a lot of people, that's a foreign concept. They think young Black kids and weapons just go together. A young Black male does not want to be in a classroom with a student who has a gun any more than the teacher does. Because that student will shoot that young Black student before he shoots a teacher."

Schools should work harder to build compassionate and respectful relationships with students, Toldson advises, so kids will feel compelled to work with school administrators instead of working against them.

"Treating all students like they are security risks brings down the school environment; it hurts education, it doesn't help it," Toldson said.

The situation is further complicated by low teacher salaries. Of the 6 million teachers in America, a good number, according to Toldson, would rather teach in more affluent districts, not only to work with the type of students they desire, but to get better salaries.

"They prefer districts where the property taxes are higher, where the homes are bigger and more expensive. Schools reap some reward for the taxes generated from wealthier districts, and that trickles down to higher teacher salaries," Toldson explained. "So a lot of them who end up in St. Louis or Washington, DC, are those who find themselves in districts that were their second, third, or fourth choice."

Some of those districts, complete with complicated layers of social and economic dysfunction, are low on teachers' "most wanted" lists, for somewhat understandable reasons, Dr. Jawanza Kunjufu points out: "If you have boys who are having challenges at home—I mean only 28 percent of our children have their fathers in the home—a lot of issues with regards to parenting, in fairness to teachers, not all teachers, white or Black, are willing to make that commitment."

Not to alienate the white teachers who represent the majority of educators in the country, Kunjufu, as an educational consultant, emphasized a strong focus on cultural competence as the area of much-needed improvement.

"In defense of white females, though, what I try to sell them on is that it's not about the race of the teacher, and not about the gender; it's expectations, time on task, and classroom management."

Being sympathetic to the challenges teachers face with Black boys and students in low-income school districts does not absolve them from confronting and correcting behaviors that cement paths to destruction for their students.

Disciplinary interventions, race-based tracking, placement in special-education classes, biased standardized tests, resentment about working in urban districts, the lack of Black male teachers in schools, ingrained stereotypes, culturally illiterate and unqualified educators with the power to classify minority students as mentally retarded—all these things should lead to several fundamental questions: Is the public school system culturally competent to teach minority children, especially already endangered Black boys? Can the public school system be reformed? If not, what alternate options should educators, parents from low-income communities, and anyone who cares pursue?

Toldson, the senior research analyst for the Congressional Black Caucus's two-part series, *Breaking Barriers: Plotting the Path to Academic Success for School-Age African-American Males*, is not a glass-half-empty sort of researcher. He takes some comfort in the fact that numerous government agencies, education experts, and major foundations have all studied the issues related to the crisis facing Black boys and low-income students. Many, he said, have taken concrete steps toward, or implemented admirable initiatives aimed at, addressing the problems. However, even Toldson recognizes that dismissive attitudes and outright disdain for Black youth has been methodically and systematically woven into the fabric of the American psyche. The backup plan, he says, is to inform and empower parents and communities so they can make school districts listen.

Jerrell, the teen who was told he'd amount to nothing in the fourth grade, made an interesting observation about "listening" during his interview. He was referring to hardheaded youth his own age, but his words are on target for a school system in need of drastic change: "It's just, are you willing to listen? Are you willing to take that positive advice that they're giving? Most people are not, though. Like, they say they're listening, but it goes through one ear and out the other."

A Few Good (Black) Men

Like so many of the boys who attend Chicago's Urban Prep Academy, Jabryce was a difficult student at his previous school, Bennett Elementary. He was always in trouble, he said. His mother was called to the school often because of her son's behavior.

"It was the girls," Jabryce admits. He spent more time trying to be "cool" than trying to behave at school.

Jabryce really is cool. And it's not because girls in his neighborhood are swooning over the good-looking kid, who has an infectious smile and big dreams for his future. The school Jabryce attends has made him quite popular: "Yeah, people, when I tell them that I go to Urban Prep, they look at me like I'm a celebrity . . . 'cause they hear about us having 100 percent of the men going to a college. I feel like that's what we're supposed to do, but other people look at it like it's a privilege, which it is . . ."

Jabryce plans to enroll at the University of Georgia after he graduates from Urban Prep. He wants to be an engineer and a "successful entrepreneur." His high school has prepared him to accomplish his goals. Mostly, he credits the male administrators and teachers at Urban Prep.

Other than his grandfather, Jabryce has had no positive male role models in his life. He has no father in the home and wagers that about "90 percent" of his schoolmates share his plight. Jabryce says his mother has always played the role of "mom and dad" in his life. Part of the reason he wants to be a success is so he can come back to Chicago and bless her with a better life. He was saved by Urban Prep, Jabryce says, and the caring, disciplined, and nurturing Black men at the school who embraced him.

"When I was in eighth grade, elementary school, I never seen Black males that were successful in life, doing something positive with their life. Here, at Urban Prep, I see it on a regular, everyday basis, and it's, like, now I know what I could be . . . I can go to college, be somebody, be successful with my life, be a positive role model for African American men."

Could turning around the lives of denied and dismissed Black boys be as simple as making sure more Black men occupy the classrooms and fill the hallways of inner-city schools?

"Yeah, I think it's essential that these guys have a diversity of positive Black male role models," said Tim King, founder and president of Urban Prep. "About 60 percent of our team is composed of African American men, and that's really driven by the fact that people really get our mission, which resonates with Black men all over the place."

Diversity trumps quantity, King stressed.

"It's important to be able to see different types of Black men getting along. I say that a lot, and I don't think people really get it. But so often, we see Black men in the media, Black men on the streets in combat with each other. Here, we've built an organization where we've got Black men—short, tall, fat, skinny, dark, light, all kinds of religions, everything."

King was also quick to refute any charges of biased recruiting.

"At Urban Prep, we don't do any race-based admissions of our students, and we don't do any race-based hiring practices at all. One of the great things about being Urban Prep and being un-apologetically Urban Prep is that folks know what we're about and people come to us. So we end up getting a really high number of African American males applying to our program to work here as teachers, as mentors, as administrators, and as staff members."

Dr. Toldson estimates that nearly 30 percent of all students in the country's public schools are white males; 7 percent are Black males. White males comprise about 16 percent of the teaching force, Black males about 1.8 percent, he says. One of the reasons males aren't flocking to the teaching profession, Toldson explains, is because most—Black, white, and other—don't consider it a viable means to support families. Even with aggressive Black male teacher recruitment, the nation will be hard-pressed to match male teacher–to–student ratios, let alone Black male student–to–teacher ratios.

Therefore, the nation is in need of a Plan B.

IT TAKES A COMMUNITY

In his landmark 2010 book, *Brainwashed: Challenging the Myth of Black Inferiority*, author and former advertising pioneer Tom Burrell offers an unsettling fact-based theory: Whites and Blacks have been subjected to 400 years of white superiority and Black inferiority conditioning.

Burrell's thesis doesn't bode well for efforts to teach cultural competency to whites if they unconsciously, consciously, or subliminally reject the notion that the inner-city neighborhoods in which they teach have value or that the kids who come out of those neighborhoods are indeed salvageable.

"Yeah, they learn that in their own grade schools and colleges," Dr. Toldson acknowledged. The deeper threat, he added, is when, on a psychological level, those teachers transfer their perceptions of inferiority onto the kids they teach.

Paul Gorski, founder of EdChange (www. edchange.org), an agency dedicated to equity, diversity, multiculturalism, and social justice in education, wrote an essay that underscored the theme of Burrell's book. One day after class, Gorski's friend Janet, an educator who teaches in an "urban Midwestern elementary classroom," sat next to him with defeat in her eyes, he wrote. Janet told Gorski that her hope was fading. Her students were smart, she said, but they were unmotivated and didn't care about school.

"And their parents," Janet continued. "I'm lucky if two or three of them show up for conferences. No wonder the kids are unprepared to learn."

Gorski, who is an assistant professor of Integrative Studies at George Mason University's New Century College, described how his friend was like many well-intentioned educators who just happened to buy into the "culture of poverty" myth, which, Gorski wrote, is the idea that poor people basically share monolithic and predictable beliefs, values, and behaviors.

Gorski refuted the popular "culture of poverty" myth and explained how, really, his friend was the one suffering from the "culture of classism."

"This culture continues to harden in our schools today. It leads the most well intentioned of us, like my friend Janet, into having low expectations for low-income students. It makes teachers fear their most powerless pupils. And worst of all, it diverts attention from what people in poverty *do* have in common: inequitable access to basic human rights."

The first step in convincing white educators that they can make a progressive difference with kids is to pull back on the negative descriptors we all use to describe Black neighborhoods and Black children, Dr. Toldson said. "Some of the information we researchers give them is really counterproductive to what we're trying to achieve. If all we're doing is giving them information related to the achievement gap and telling them about crime, drugs, and violence in the communities that these kids are coming from, I think it leads them to be more apathetic, more anxious, and less effective.

"The responsibility of researchers, filmmakers, and public figures," Toldson said, "is to help educators gain a better perspective of the kids they work with and to find ways to make 'the genius' realistic in their minds. Don't just show the problems; show them their capacity to be whatever they want to be, or whatever society wants them to be, given the right support."

Toldson also insisted that school systems be held accountable for providing the cultural-competence training teachers need.

"Schools have a budget to provide various resources for their teachers. We need to make sure teachers know about the characteristics of the kids they're working with, their learning styles, and their resilience. Teachers have to learn how to accommodate the working style of the holistic learner, who may not learn in a linear fashion. They need to make sure there are no biases in the material that they're giving students. It may sound like a lot to do, but it's really not. Schools already have the structure in place for some degree of in-service training. They just have to tailor that training to meet the needs of the students they serve."

William C. Wade, former principal of Roberts Vaux High School, a Promise Academy in Philadelphia—another inner-city school, like Urban Prep, that has received praise for its success with disadvantaged kids—said that he's willing to help teachers who want help: "Now, if you got in this business and you're not really sure what you were getting into, I'm here to support you. I can send you to professional development; I can help you. I can train you to be a great teacher. But if you're stuck in your ways and you don't want to learn, you should go."

Dr. Jawanza Kunjufu offered common-sense remedies that go beyond race. The United States has 500 single-gender classrooms and more than 100 single-gender schools. Those schools and best-case examples of single-gender environments practiced in countries like Belgium, Germany, and Switzerland offer possible models for raceless intervention, Kunjufu suggested. "If you know that girls mature faster than boys—almost a three-year difference—then instead of placing boys in special education, we should allow for those differences or consider single-gender classrooms. Accommodations can include shortening lesson plans, allowing more movement in the classroom, and holding physical education classes daily. If you know that girls are more verbal, then allow for the possibility that boys will not only communicate differently, but will also express an interest in reading a little later than girls," Kunjufu said.

The crisis that Black boys and other youth face in the nation is indeed immense. When accessing the multifaceted problems, which include biased testing and disproportionate disciplinary actions aimed at Black boys, Tavis Smiley acknowledged that white Americans must be fully engaged in tackling educational problems. However, during the taping of his PBS special, Smiley also challenged interviewees to address the flip side of the equation: "How seriously are Black folk taking this crisis?"

It was a question Urban Prep's Tim King has pondered. "That's one of the concerns I have when I look broadly at the issues our race, and African American boys in particular, are facing," King said. "What I'm viewing is that some haves are not really focusing on the have-nots. You know, it's 'I got mine and I'm going to make sure my kids got theirs, but I'm not going to worry about the folks in the neighborhood that my mother or my grandmother lived in.' I think, as African Americans," King continued, "we have to look very closely at ourselves and what we're doing as a people to help our communities."

Dr. Ivory Toldson, of Howard University, welcomed the question also. He suggested that "communities," which may comprise many races, build relationships with schools that allow them to express how they want Black boys to be treated. Empowered communities, Toldson said, don't *ask* that teachers receive cultural competency training—they *demand* it.

"Communities and parents have a big role to play in just being present and making sure all our students are treated with respect. When a school is suspending a kid every week for coming to school late and is not taking the time to find out *why* that kid is coming to school late, then that's a problem. That's something the community needs to address."

"Community" is big at Urban Prep. "It can also be a big tool for change," Tim King suggested. "At Urban Prep, I think we've been real lucky. We have an African American board, and we have a lot of Black professionals who are engaged in solving this problem and trying to move forward this notion that, you know, we are one community and we have a responsibility to our community.

"It's a message we try to communicate to our students as well. But I think, more broadly, Black people have not been as attentive to that piece, and we need to be. We need to be."

CHAPTER 4

I DON'T SEE

It was one of those unexpected moments of deep revelation.

Walter Dean Myers wasn't expecting anything special as he boarded the train on that particular morning. The author, who has written more than 100 books, is perhaps the most dominant African American voice in young adult literature. Myers's work reflects the lives of young Black people—the places they live; the sports they play; the struggles, letdowns, and triumphs they navigate; and the insecurities they shoulder from living in homes without fathers and in neighborhoods without safety. There probably isn't a school library in the country that doesn't have Myers's signature work, *Monster*, on its shelves.

On the train, a young girl, head down, was caught up in a Walter Dean Myers book. She had no idea the author, just seats away, was quietly watching and enjoying her absorption in his work.

"And then she stopped and just looked up in the air," Myers recalled, as he shared the incident with Tavis Smiley. "And I knew, for that moment, I was occupying her mind.

"My stories don't have to be good stories. All they have to be is stories, which reflect their lives. That's all it has to be . . . if it reflects their lives, they will find a way to go through that book. And . . . that's all that it takes."

Myers knows he is blessed with a rare gift. Through his work, he can capture the minds of young people. He can help them see themselves outside the narrow and negative prisms mass media reserves for those who look like them. Without finger pointing or pontificating, Myers has given hundreds of thousands of young people, some whose dreams have been crushed, the license to dream anyway.

"I know where these kids are coming from. I know what they're going through. I know how it feels to be a young Black teenager. When I include them in my books—and not just with a Black face, but with the full spectrum of their lives—I think this is what they're looking for."

Myers has successfully chronicled the lives of disadvantaged Black youth, especially boys, because that was his life too. Two years after his birth in 1937, Walter Milton Myers was given to Herbert and Florence Dean, an African American man and a woman of German and Native American descent. To this day, Myers writes on his Web site (www.walterdeanmyers.net), he's not sure why his birth parents gave him away. But he loved the Deans dearly and assumed the last name of his adoptive parents.

Myers was raised in Harlem, which he loved. He met Langston Hughes and James Baldwin in his own neighborhood. Myers said he was a very bright child for the first 13 years of his life, until his "family began to fall apart."

In the midst of family turmoil, Myers went from being a "bright" child to a distracted and troubled student. He was quick-tempered and got into fights often. Still, Myers had developed an early appetite for books. He'd bring them home from libraries wrapped in brown paper bags to avoid being teased by neighborhood boys who preyed on bookish types.

Eventually, Myers decided to drop out of high school. Teachers and counselors tried to intervene. They wanted to help, but Myers didn't feel comfortable opening up and sharing his personal pain with them. "The counselors asked me what was wrong . . . I wasn't going to tell some teacher that my mom is an alcoholic—I wasn't going to do that," Myers said.

A high school teacher encouraged Myers to write. He did and enjoyed it. Myers considered himself a fairly decent writer. Even though he was determined to drop out at the age of 16, his teacher encouraged him to keep writing, no matter what happened in his life. "It's what you do," Myers said, recalling the teacher's advice.

Myers joined the Army at the age of 17. When he got out four years later, he tried to figure out what a young man with no high school diploma could do with his life. One day, while working on a construction site, the teacher's words came back to him. "So I tried writing, and I enjoyed it, not because I made any money at it, but rather because it made me feel better about myself."

The rest, as they say, is history. But Myers has never forgotten how reading, writing, and words impacted his life and career. He spends countless hours in schools, juvenile detention centers, and libraries, trying to share what he knows about books with young people. Myers is a staunch believer in the transformative power of books, but he's also keenly aware of the damage wrought by literature that does not reflect the lives of Black youth.

As a child in the 1950s, Myers was exposed only to white and British authors. When he met Langston Hughes in Harlem, he didn't consider the legendary author and poet a "real writer," because Hughes wasn't white, Myers recalled during a 2008 National Public Radio interview. "I didn't see myself represented in any of the reading material. And I understand, as other kids do, that when they go to school, books transmit values. And if I'm not in those books, what are you saying about my values?"

If he had been exposed to books "which included my life," Myers said, he would have finished high school and gone on to college. That simple but powerful recognition motivates him to talk to as many educators and school administrators as possible.

"When I visit schools and tell teachers that I dropped out of school at 16, and there were things going on in my life—you know, people were being arrested, my uncle got murdered, my mom was an alcoholic—they don't believe that. They say, 'Well, okay, how are you this successful?'"

Too many Black kids, especially Black boys, believe "success is *not* for them," Myers says. They come to school from environments that reinforce this disbelief. However, he stresses, Black kids are just as intelligent as white kids. Teachers and educational institutions need to understand that they can reach Black boys with literature if that material reflects their lives and experiences.

"What was it about education . . . going to school, going to class, that made you *not* interested in the first place?"

The small, U-shaped group of boys seemed to appreciate the fact that Tavis Smiley, a "celebrity," a guy who's on TV, was sincerely interested in their lives and opinions. They answered questions as if they had been waiting a long time for someone finally to ask. "Well, some of it got to do with, like, we weren't interested in the things they were teaching and everything . . . and then the teachers didn't want to teach and stuff like that," offered a young detainee.

Another kid, wearing a blue sweatshirt, his dreadlocks swept back and bound at the back of his head by a fat rubber band, described the factors in his life that caused his attention to drift from teachers and school.

"Because, like, when I grew up . . . when I was eight . . . not going to school, and getting suspended, kicked out, getting sent back home and stuff like that," the boy in blue answered.

Smiley pressed for specifics: "You weren't paying attention because you were focused on what?"

"My sister's murder," the boy said matter-of-factly.

After a second of stunned silence, Smiley invited the boys to open up and talk about the psychic effects of violence: "How many boys are traumatized in that way?"

"Most of them," replied the boy who lost his sister. "Watching someone die, getting shot or something, seeing a murder, someone with a gun, stuff like that . . ." he said, then paused to allow a boy in a black sweatshirt to chime in.

"I was going to say the same thing . . . every day somebody getting shot . . . [It's] for real."

Walter Dean Myers is concerned about Black boys and low-income youth who are exposed to daily negativities in their communities before they even leave their homes for school. Books like his can help them feel less alone and isolated, and can draw them into worlds of literature that reflect their lives and neighborhoods. However, getting past the trauma is a major challenge in homes without fathers and schools without the structural resources to address Black boys' psychological needs.

According to the 2007 U.S. Census report "Custodial Mothers and Fathers and Their Child Support," there are approximately 13.6 million single parents in the United States responsible for raising 21.2 million children under the age of 21.

The long-term effects of more than 20 million children "who go to bed every night without a hug or kiss from dad" leaves a psychological scar on Black boys and accounts for much of the "drama and trauma impacting the 'hood daily," wrote David Miller, M.Ed., cofounder of the Urban Leadership Institute, a Baltimore, Maryland–based nonprofit advocacy group for youth. Legendary but troubled rappers such as Tupac Shakur, Biggie Smalls, Eminem, and Jay-Z—all of whom echo the "unresolved pain that comes from being part of the 'absent daddy club,'" Miller said—should erase any doubt that "growing up without a father leaves an indelible impression on young boys."

There are a handful of organizations such as Raising Him Alone (www.raisinghimalone.com) that provide information and resources to help single mothers raise Black boys. However, much of the data, research, and hands-on material that specifically address the psychic trauma Black boys in disadvantaged communities struggle with has not been delivered to schools or parents.

Even without packaged institutional resources, however, some school administrators, teachers, and parents have came up with their own common-sense, "old-school," and practical ways to get Black boys reading, writing, communicating, and excelling in school.

If schools are going to get serious about bringing change to the lives of Black boys, they need to "make everybody in your community a part of the community," said Woolworth V. Davis, principal at Ethel Allen Elementary School, another Promise Academy in Philadelphia.

The advice is rooted in Davis's entrée into education. After college, he became a teacher but bailed on the profession. "The kids were a challenge, and I didn't think I was ready," he has said. Davis became the building engineer at a high school, basically spending his days "working in a boiler room and cleaning up the school." Somehow, though, that engineer wound up delivering the commencement address at the school's graduation.

As the engineer/maintenance man, Davis was able to engage students on a different level. Through conversations, he learned about the neighborhoods they came from and the lives they led. It was an exchange between a teacher and student that cemented his decision to return to the profession. One day, he watched a student give a dozen roses to a teacher. The teacher cried, he said. Observing that act of gratitude, he came to a powerful realization: "I said, you know what, that's the reward. You're never going to get rich in this profession, but when you can change a child's life, that's the reward. So I said to myself, 'Let me go back to school.'"

Davis went back to school to earn his master's degree but was still an engineer when the principal asked him to deliver the school's commencement address. Later, he pursued his administrative degree, and, several years and promotions following that, he went on to become vice principal and principal at other schools before he was named principal of Ethel Allen Elementary.

As principal, Davis employs the same engagement practices he had honed as an engineer.

When kids arrive at Ethel Allen, they are greeted by the principal, who insists they shake his hand every morning.

Davis said he sees the problems from home etched on some of the boys' faces. "So I greet them, 'How you doin', man,' and I tell them I need a firm handshake. We make them feel good, with a happy smile and a 'good morning.' The important part of all this is to engage them for learning in the classroom. And that learning has to be relevant. You gotta make it real. You can't talk about things that they cannot relate to."

It's all about discipline and communication, Davis says.

The kids attend town-hall meetings at the school, where they debate, perform, or speak from the stage. In order to get them to communicate their feelings, Davis encourages students to get comfortable with public speaking before audiences of their peers and teachers. "I believe speaking in front of people is very important. Our kids are beat down, so we have to teach them to speak with their heads up—look me in my eye."

The school was "off the hook" when he arrived in 2010, with kids running in the hallways, kicking in the doors, yelling, and screaming.

"You the new principal?" one boisterous child asked on his first day.

"I said, 'Boy, sit back down,'" Davis recalled with a laugh. "That's the way you have to deal with them. Let them know that you mean what you say and you say what you mean, and they'll respect you."

Davis summarized his program for his students thus: "Discipline, communication, academics, how to live and respect."

"They don't get it in the neighborhood anymore," Davis said. "When I was coming up, guys in the neighborhood, even the alcoholics, the drug dealers, didn't matter. They had respect.

"I have a lot of young Caucasian teachers, and they're good teachers, but they need to understand the child that we're teaching. So I also have a few good men—these guys are from the 'hood. They come in and they know the boys. They see them daily in the neighborhoods, and give them the benefit of their knowledge."

Although he doesn't tolerate any "talking down" or "finger pointing" when dealing with his students, Davis cautions teachers not to pity his students: "Don't feel sorry for them, don't pamper them; teach them to be responsible." If a boy "acts out," Davis says, he has instructed teachers to first investigate the triggers that caused them to get out of control, then to try to deescalate those motivators. Second, he tells his staff to give kids, especially misbehaving boys, something constructive to do. Have an extracurricular activity or a lesson prepared for them every day. Because boys dealing with boredom or off-campus challenges need structure, he explained.

"I try to impress upon my staff to make them live up to their responsibility. Kids need love, but I hate seeing that 'Come on, baby' stuff. No, don't do that. Talk to him about what needs to be done, and then let him go on and change his behaviors."

Tough love, discipline, and constant personal communication are just a few of the tiers on Davis's educational ladder. As with other Promise Academies, a full staff of counselors, social workers, and other professionals are on hand to address the emotional and mental health needs of the children.

Davis is acutely aware that public schools need more Black males. To that end, he made a personal appeal asking Black men to consider the profession: "Our young men need you; they need

African American role models. They need to see how you walk, dress, and conduct yourselves. So just come and try it for a minute. See how you can benefit yourself and benefit young men. Like me, I think you will love it."

GIVING THEM SOMETHING THEY CAN FEEL

Wade and Cheryl Hudson staked their claim in the "making a difference" arena over 25 years ago. The Hudsons understood how important it is that Black children see their images and hear their own stories.

When the Hudsons couldn't find the variety of rich stories and illustrations they knew would ignite young minds, spark imaginations, and instill pride, they defied short-sighted mainstream publishers who rejected their manuscripts with claims that there was no market for Black children's books. In 1988, they founded Just Us Books, a company solely dedicated to Black children's book publishing. Their first release, *AFRO-BETS® ABC Book*, taught the alphabet using African American themes and children's images. With limited funds and an aggressive grassroots campaign, the trailblazers sold 5,000 copies in three months. Numerous best-selling and award-winning titles later, the Hudsons have become a lighthouse for children and young adult readers.

So how do we ensnare Black boys in the wonderful web of reading? The Hudsons answer this question in the latest edition of the Just Us Books newsletter (http://justusbooks.com). They teach us that boys tend to shy away from stories about girls; boys are collectors who gravitate toward books in series form; boys prefer books that reflect the things they do or want to do, such as sports and other hobbies, whereas girls read more fiction; boys like humorous books, science fiction, fantasy, and escapism.

The Hudsons urge parents not to ridicule or put their boys down if they like comic books or picture magazines instead of novels and chapter books. The important thing is to nurture reading. In fact, fathers are encouraged to indulge their inner child and read comics or graphic novels with their boys. Since boys like reading material in series and emulate the men in their lives, a father who's excited about the next adventure of the newly debuted multicultural *Spider-Man*, Miles Morales, a character who is Black and Hispanic, or who is willing to explore the provocative world of

Aaron MacGruder's *Boondocks* may have planted the seeds for a boy's first home library.

Fathers and male caregivers should read with their boys, have them read aloud to them, and equally important, they should try to let boys see them reading books. Black boys attend schools where more than 80 percent of the teachers are white females. They need to see Black men that they love reading.

Allow boys to choose their own reading material, advised the Hudsons. Unlike girls, boys have a difficult time walking into a book store or library because they are not as communicative about their choices. Encouraging boys to pick and choose their own material can help boost their confidence. Usually, mothers choose the books for the family. The Hudsons suggest a shift.

Before a child turns 18, they will have seen 360,000 commercials. It's a safe bet these images will come via cell phones, iPads, iPods, or some new form of electronic device. How many positive images of Black boys will be reflected in the new mediums of the digital revolution? Will their history, stories, and real life experiences get lost in transition?

The Game of Life

It's hard to believe that *Grand Theft Auto*, a popular but violent video game, was the seed that sprouted an innovative program and is the gateway for a brand new way for Black boys to see and express themselves.

Believe it. During a symposium on video game design in 2004, Roderick Woodruff, an advertising and IT professional, found himself debating with gamers about *Grand Theft Auto*. Was the Black protagonist in the game cast in a stereotypical racist light or not? Then someone asked: "Well, where are the video games that portray minorities in a positive light, as positive role models?"

For Woodruff, someone who's deeply concerned about the African American achievement gap, the question brought to mind several compelling facts: Black kids spend millions on video games; Black people are rarely represented positively in those games; video game production is composed of critical 21st-century educational components, i.e. STEM (science, technology, engineering, and mathematics), and Woodruff, a passionate storyteller, had a strong desire to teach boys, especially Black boys, how to tell their stories through the new technology.

Those facts became the foundation of the Urban Video Game Academy (UVGA), an after-school and summer program that teaches middle and high school urban youth the basics of video game development. "Every boy has a story," Woodruff says, describing how his program connects students with their history, culture, identity, and values. "I ask the boys, 'Who are you?' because 'who you are' is directly connected to your grandparents, your neighbors, where you live, who you love or hate and all of your experiences. I want each student to see himself as a whole person with a unique set of experiences and then be able to use the technology to translate their story into a video game."

There are many rewards in exposing Black boys to their true reflections at public charter schools in the Washington and Baltimore areas, Woodruff said. Giving them and other underserved kids the opportunity to experience an innovative, high-tech program that can't be found in cash-strapped urban schools or elite, well-funded high schools is a special gift.

"At the heart of UVGA is the opportunity to show our boys how they can turn their light on from the inside. I teach them how to ask 'why?'

and watch their minds expand and grow until they build enough competence and confidence to ask 'why not?' That's how dreams become reality."

CHAPTER 5

DISMANTLING THE PRESCHOOL-TO-

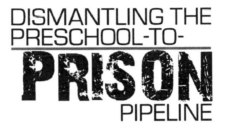

PRISON
PIPELINE

At 17, Jonathan Roach finally gets it. He understands why people told him to read books when he was a child. When he was younger, he didn't see the point. Through books and reading, Jonathan now understands the history and struggles of African Americans—the people who share his hue and experiences. Today, Jonathan believes he has value.

"I was, like, 'I don't wanna read that.' That's how my mind-set was then. Now that I started reading . . . it's like, 'Wow,' this is very interesting. Just to know what I know . . . it's like, 'Oh, we was not just slaves, like we actually came from somewhere; we were somebody?' Learning them type of things just opened my eyes, like, 'Yeah, it's more to this.'"

Jonathan found something missing from his education as a child: "It's kinda like a joke; you'd go to school, and it's like nothing was really interesting, you know, nothing was about me. I'm very interested in myself and my background, my history; and nothing was about me, so I really wasn't interested in the classes that were given."

Jonathan now sees a promising future for himself as a college graduate with a degree in psychology, counseling other troubled youth and teaching them about their history and their worth.

But first he has to complete a four-year sentence that started at the Alameda County Juvenile Justice Center in 2009 and, with good behavior, will end at a state prison—he thinks San Quentin—in 2013.

Jonathan is not unlike many other kids who grew up in Oakland, California, where the crime rate is three times the national average. He dropped out of school in ninth grade. At the age of 15, he was arrested for possession of an illegal firearm and was sent to juvenile detention for two months. Just when he was about to finish probation for that charge, Jonathan got into trouble again—serious trouble. He was arrested, charged, and convicted of two counts of armed robbery, two counts of kidnapping, and two counts of assault with a deadly weapon. Those charges led to his being tried as an adult. He will remain in juvenile custody until his 18th birthday, which at the time of this writing was only a few months away. Once he turns 18, he will be transferred to state prison, where he'll serve out the remainder of his four-year sentence.

Jonathan's situation mirrors that of more than 2,000 teens who, on any given day, are detained or under the supervision of the California Juvenile Justice System. Many, like Jonathan, are repeat offenders. This is particularly true for low-performing readers.

Jonathan was one of the incarcerated juveniles Tavis Smiley interviewed for *Too Important to Fail*. The dimpled, charismatic youth with short dreadlocks spoke confidently about his plans to get his GED and then get a college degree; he wants to change his life and become a positive force with low-income kids.

"I'm gon' open up a big recreation center, and just sit down and talk to them, like, y'all can be somebody, too," Jonathan explained. With obvious bravado, he spoke of his ability to carry out his plans:

"It takes someone strong, like I consider myself, you know, strong."

The host reminded Jonathan that he'll soon leave a "place with a bunch of youngsters to be with a bunch of men" in San Quentin. When he asked Jonathan if he was mentally prepared for the transition to adult prison, the Teflon veneer faded and the voice of a 17-year-old wavered: "Not yet. I believe that it hasn't dawned on me yet. Like, or maybe I will never be scared. I don't know, it's kinda like in our neighborhood, it's like prison . . . it's the norm."

David Muhammad, who was named head of Alameda County Probation Department in early 2011, is disturbed by what Jonathan and other Black youth consider the "norm" in their communities. "What most of the young people in my facility grow up in are environments of destruction—environments with concentrated poverty, blighted neighborhoods, substandard schools, high unemployment, a liquor store on every corner, drugs readily available, and guns easily accessible. If that's your environment, destructive behavior is almost common or normal."

Stressing that teens must be held accountable for their actions, Muhammad added: "But most young people come into the system as a result of some trauma that they experienced. So if I'm a 15-year-old boy and I saw my best friend shot and killed in the street and my aunt died of AIDS and I've never met my dad and my mom works two jobs just to keep food on the table and I'm frustrated and traumatized over those life circumstances and then I start smoking weed and cutting class, and then I may even steal a car . . . how should we respond to that young person? Should we just punish him for his behavior? Or should we recognize the trauma that he's experienced and try to address that trauma?"

Very few experts dispute the direct correlation between high school dropout rates and prison populations. Most agree that the less time a boy spends in high school, the more time he'll spend incarcerated. There may be conflicting ideas about how to save public education, but there is little disagreement that Black boys who are disproportionately represented in juvenile corrections facilities need immediate salvation.

Race and poverty are consistent similarities in the lives of Black boys caught up in the criminal justice system, said Muhammad. But the similarity they all share relates to education, or the lack thereof.

"The biggest thing that predicts a child's being in a California prison is that he dropped out or he has low educational achievement."

Marian Wright Edelman, president of the Washington, DC–based Children's Defense Fund, bluntly defines "America's pipeline to prison" as the "worst crisis faced by millions of Black children since slavery." Her assessment doesn't seem far from reality when considering the facts found in the organization's *Portrait of Inequality 2011* report:

- Nationally, Black youth are more than four times as likely as white youth to be detained in a juvenile correctional facility. About two-thirds are detained for nonviolent offenses.

- In 2008, Blacks constituted 17 percent of the youth population (age 10 to 17), yet they constituted 31 percent of all juvenile arrests.

- Between the ages of 10 and 17, Black youth are five times as likely as a white youth to be arrested for a violent crime.

- Black males born in 2001 are more than five times as likely as white males to be incarcerated some time in their lifetime.

- Black males age 18 and over in 2008 represented only 5 percent of the total college student population, but 36 percent of the total prison population.

Models for Change, a national initiative established to accelerate the reform of juvenile justice systems, notes the racial ramifications of a short-sighted and primarily punitive juvenile correctional system on its Web site at www.modelsfor change.net: "Youth of color are overrepresented at nearly every point of contact with the juvenile justice system—and this 'disproportionate minority contact' is disturbingly persistent over time. Youth of color are more likely to be incarcerated and to serve more time than white youth, even when they are charged with the same category of offense."

Various studies verify that poor Black children attend the worst educational facilities with the least resources, and are taught by inexperienced and unqualified teachers who have low expectations for their Black and Latino students. The pipeline from schools to prison is one in which poor and minority children are held back en masse, subjected to out-of-school suspensions, and sequestered in special-education classes throughout their years in school. All this, the Children's Defense Fund report concludes, contributes to "student discouragement, low self-esteem, and general disengagement from school."

Dr. Jawanza Kunjufu argues that a major factor in the disproportionately high representation of Black boys in intervention programs like special education is because there has been no accommodation for "gender differences in learning styles." Considering that 83 percent of the nation's teachers are white and female, could it be that "the ideal student, the norm, the benchmark, is the white female student?" Kunjufu asks.

To reinforce his point about the reasons behind the disproportionate number of Black male students in special-education programs, Kunjufu suggests a study of the "behaviors and attributes" profile of the "ideal student":

- Quiet
- Can sit still for long periods of time
- A long attention span
- Can work independently
- Likes ditto sheets
- A left-brain learner
- Passive
- Speaks standard English
- Two-parent home
- Learned reading before second grade
- Well-developed fine motor skills

"When you compare this list with the attributes of male students and factor in the learning styles and culture of African American children," Kunjufu wrote in an essay for the Web site Teachers of Color, "it is easier to understand why African American children represent only 17 percent of the school population but constitute more than

30 percent of the children in special education. It also becomes apparent why African American males represent almost 80 percent of African American children placed."

During a 1998 interview with NPR, Geoffrey Canada, founder of the Harlem Children's Zone, reflected on the nation's focus on the development of girls at that time. He specifically cited efforts such as the Take Our Daughters to Work program founded in 1993 by Gloria Steinem and the Ms. Foundation for Women. "But I look at these boys. The consequences of poor boys, when we don't do a good job, is that they die, they go to prison, they are maimed and scarred for life," Canada said.

When one factors in that more than 1 million young men under 18 are caught up in the penal system and are boys growing up without fathers, the negative conclusions are clear, said Canada. "Well, it's because we are not doing a good job with these boys. And I'm telling you, these boys are in a lot of trouble in our country."

With more and more schools serving as de facto correctional facilities, the school-to-prison pipeline is guaranteed a consistent flow. The link between disciplinary practices at schools and the juvenile justice system has been thoroughly dissected in studies like "Breaking Barriers: Plotting the Path to Academic Success for School-Age African-American Males," released by the Congressional Black Caucus Foundation. Zero-tolerance policies and the use of law enforcement to address minor disciplinary problems, the report cites, has ultimately led to the rise in the number of juvenile inmates.

Jonathan's route from a predictable path to a promising future came through the efforts of David Muhammad, an unapologetic reformer who has made it his priority to separate kids with promise from proven incorrigibles. Juvenile offenders are still held absolutely accountable, but Muhammad works to provide the self-improvement, education, and job-skills training needed for these young men to become truly rehabilitated, functioning members of society. Because of Muhammad's program, Jonathan started reading and now believes he can positively influence other Black youth.

Muhammad's life story serves as the bedrock of his belief that juveniles can be rehabilitated—if someone invests the attention and resources necessary to make it outside "the system." As a teen from a broken home, he was arrested three times—for drug possession and attempted murder. He was spared because no charges were filed in those cases, but Muhammad realizes how perilously close he came to being another young Black statistic trapped in "the system" he now runs.

"I was raised in Oakland, California, single mother, had two brothers growing up, one started using drugs, one started selling drugs before I was done with elementary school. So you know, those were my examples," Muhammad recalls. "Unfortunately, by the time I got to high school, I was in the foster care system, in the juvenile justice system, and making bad decisions—been arrested a few times, was on probation in Alameda County. Ultimately, it was being around the wrong people, not interested in school, and having too much access to negative influences."

In 1987, Muhammad's girlfriend took him to the Omega Boys Club, a nonprofit youth agency in San Francisco. There, caring adults counseled and nurtured the troubled youth. The organization even covered Muhammad's college tuition at Howard University.

After graduation, he paid the gift forward, accepting a job as director of counseling programs at the Oakland Mentoring Center. Then he moved on to work for New York City's probation department. In 2009, after relocating to Washington, DC, to work for the district's Department of Youth Rehabilitating Services, Muhammad established New Beginnings, a program that offers counseling and educational resources and alternatives for youth facing incarceration.

It makes no difference if it's labeled irony or destiny, Muhammad considers it his duty to provide troubled youth—particularly Black boys—the attention, care, and resources they need to get off the track that leads to lifelong imprisonment.

Little changes here or there, Muhammad says, won't do. Far from naïve, he admits, "I run a probation department that for the moment often makes young people worse, not better." In reality, he adds, the school-to-prison pipeline constitutes a "state of emergency" in need of complete overhaul.

Tracing the Pipeline

In his interview with Smiley, Jonathan excitedly described the two African American studies classes he was taking at the time. Through classes like those, he said, he came to understand that he was a willing participant in an age-old conspiracy to contain Black men. "It's like, if I knew what I know now, I really wouldn't be here. I mean, the prison industrial complex and Black America . . . the things that they do to target us . . . it's very eye-opening and enlightening. . . . If I knew what I know now, I wouldn't have fell for what I did."

After prodding from Smiley, Jonathan admitted that, ultimately, he allowed himself to become a pawn in a system that disregards Black life. Still, if Americans are dedicated to dismantling the pipeline that leads Black boys and other minority youth from schools to prisons, a trek through the nation's past might be in order to gauge the full scope of an embedded problem.

The predestined course of mass incarceration, especially for Black boys, is an issue that legal scholar, civil rights advocate, and author Michelle Alexander details in her speeches and her highly acclaimed book, *The New Jim Crow: Mass Incarceration in the Age of Colorblindness*. The crisis facing Black youth today was one seeded in American society centuries ago and was accelerated by an aggressive "war on drugs" targeting communities of color, Alexander argues.

In his 2009 NAACP centennial celebration speech, President Obama urged parents to convince children that their destinies are in their hands, and that crime, poverty, or gang violence are "no excuses" for earning bad grades or for dropping out of school.

Telling young boys in ghetto communities that "destiny is in your hands" may make for a good sound bite, but for many Black boys, "it may turn out to be a lie," Alexander said during a March 2010 interview with *Democracy Now!*

The author challenged President Obama's statement, saying, "The rules and laws that govern ghetto communities today and the war that is being waged there ensures that a large majority of Black and brown boys in those communities will be branded as felons, labeled as criminals, at very young ages, often before they even reach voting age, before they turn eighteen. The drug war waged in poor communities of color has created generations of Black and brown people who have been branded felons and relegated to permanent second-class status for life."

Echoing Marian Wright Edelman's comparison, she underscores the painful reality that in 21st-century America, "there are more African Americans under correctional control, whether in prison or in jail, on probation or on parole, than there were enslaved in the year 1850."

In the same interview, Alexander discussed sinister economic and political benefits derived from keeping Black boys behind bars. Many old and some new prisons are located in rural areas. The majority of people warehoused in those prisons are poor people of color who lose their right to vote. The way census laws and redistricting operates in the United States, wherever people are warehoused, they count as part of the local population. Alexander explained how this scheme allows greater numbers of state representatives to be assigned to rural communities:

"And additional federal funding flows to those communities because their population has been inflated due to such large prison populations."

Meanwhile, the poor communities of color suffer a population decline because prisoners have been extracted. Communities of color lose representation and possible funding, which flows instead to rural white communities, whose populations have swelled from the mass imprisonment of Blacks and people of color.

Kunjufu laments the "economic connection" between special-education programs and new prison construction: "How unfortunate it is that we believe it is better to incarcerate someone at $28,000 per year rather than teach a child to read for less than $1,000." The connection, he adds, "is the 80 percent of special-education students labeled as reading and writing deficient and the 50 percent of students diagnosed with ADD and ADHD placed in special-education programs."

All the old forms of discrimination in employment, housing, access to education and public benefits, and voting rights are perfectly legal once individuals are branded "felons," Michelle Alexander says. This legal discrimination reinforces a racial caste system in America. It's a system, she insists, that places children of color at extreme disadvantage from birth.

TURNING DEFICITS INTO ASSETS

David Muhammad is an advocate of exploring the past to chart a better course for the future. What attracted him to Jonathan was the young man's resilient attitude. That attitude, he says, is alive and well in Black communities throughout the country. Programs and curricula should be developed so that Black kids can connect with the resilience inherent in their unique American story, Muhammad adds. "We've got to engage these young people, because many of them have many assets, many strengths. And we've got to focus on those assets, not just their deficits. That circles back to improving the education system, improving access to services that develop their strengths within their communities."

Muhammad's current college program is a condensed version of the one he started with New Beginnings while working in Washington, DC. The effort grew to a point at which his former organization sent 25 youths from juvenile facilities to colleges. So far, Muhammad has personally committed to sending at least two kids to college through his pilot program until the probation department officially adopts and funds an expanded version.

Two kids out of two thousand won't effect immediate change in California or in any other state's broken juvenile justice system. Thankfully, however, several organizations are waging battles on various fronts.

Much of the crisis involving young Black boys is also directly related to the absence of Black men—in homes, communities, and schools. It's a sad but true fact that only 1.7 percent of the nation's 4.8 million teachers in public schools are African American men. During his interview with Smiley, Jonathan pondered the outcome of having a Black male teacher in his life: "Me personally, no, I've never had a Black [teacher], nah. It would've made a big difference. I believe Black men would have actually taken the time to, you know, explain certain things to me . . . it's certain things that you have to know as a Black man that you should teach younger Black men."

The 100 Black Men of America understands this. The organization has a network of chapters, located across the United States and internationally, that offer programs such as the agency's Mentoring the 100 Way as well as other holistic programs developed to address the social, emotional, and cultural needs of children aged 8 through 18.

Trained and certified mentors, advocates, and role models within specific communities offer one-on-one and group mentoring, self-identity, and life-skills services in an attempt to forge ongoing relationships with young people. Black boys are a particular focus of 100 Black Men of America.

Trying to strengthen its efforts to reduce racial and ethnic disparities in the juvenile justice system, the nonprofit Models for Change launched the Disproportionate Minority Contact Action Network in 2007. The initiative was created to expose those working within the juvenile justice systems across the country to the latest data and research on reducing minority and ethnic youth contact with the juvenile detention facilities.

In her September 4, 2009, commentary, "Promising Models for Reforming Juvenile Justice Systems," Marian Wright Edelman cites several programs that seem to be working across the country. For example, she credits the state of Missouri's unique "rehabilitative and therapeutic approach" to overhauling its juvenile justice system. According to national figures, Missouri's juvenile recidivism rate has only 8 percent of those incarcerated coming back into juvenile custody. Missouri's success, Edelman writes, could serve as a national model for treating youth "as potentially productive members of society instead of lost causes in a prison cage."

In March 2011, filmmaker Spike Lee, Education Secretary Arne Duncan, and MSNBC contributor Jeff Johnson teamed up to encourage Black male college graduates to go into teaching. The town-hall event, held at Morehouse College, was part of the Department of Education's TEACH campaign (teach.gov), which aspires to engage all Americans in the battle to improve the nation's classrooms.

At the event, Johnson promoted his "5 by 2015" (5by2015.org) initiative and his goal to "increase the number of Black male teachers nationally to 5 percent by 2015." Those figures come to about 80,000 Black male teachers joining the educational ranks in the next four years.

Lee, a Morehouse college alumnus, reminisced about the two Black male educators who motivated him to "do the right thing" in school and after he graduated. The filmmaker encouraged the mostly Black audience to use any means necessary to get Black men engaged with Black boys: "Everybody can't be a business major. We have to educate ourselves. We have to educate our young Black men!"

Even though he's serving time within the juvenile detention center, 17-year-old Jonathan Roach is doing his part: "My unit's full of young Black men, so we all talk; we all tell each other a lot. Everything that I know, I'm telling somebody else, and hopefully, they're telling somebody else, 'cause it's mostly us up in here—young Black men."

CHAPTER 6

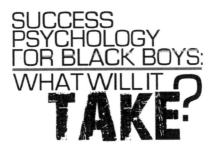

SUCCESS PSYCHOLOGY FOR BLACK BOYS: WHAT WILL IT TAKE?

Dwayne, the ebony-hued football-player-sized youth, finger-twirled the ends of his dreadlocks during the group discussion at the Alameda County Juvenile Hall. The finger wove around a lock even as he talked about the rationale that sent him back to "juvy" for selling drugs: "I'm still seventeen . . . I ain't got nowhere to go and it's all I know. That's fast money, that's cash money. So when you get out you . . . every time I got out, I had a couple of dollars but it wasn't like what I wanted.

"That's why people end up back in the system because they're listening but not listening. They gave me three and half months or something, you feel me? When I got out, my family was there, but I didn't have nothing. So I went and I got back out there and did the same thing. I ain't going to lie, I started doing the same thing because I need the money."

If we are honest, we can see that in the material world in which we live, a lot of kids like Dwayne need the money. They are bombarded 24/7 with media messages that convince them that their identities depend upon the jeans, jackets, and shoes they wear. The "bling-bling" lifestyles that hypnotize kids across class and economic lines work to convince them that they must get rich or die trying. Yet society acts surprised that these kids will do whatever it takes to achieve these lifestyles and hurt whoever gets in the way of their warped pursuit of the American Dream.

Michelle Alexander, author of *The New Jim Crow: Mass Incarceration in the Age of Colorblindness*, has written and spoken candidly about the revolving door of the criminal justice system that spins kids like Dwayne smack-dab back in the middle of the American nightmare. In fact, it has become politically profitable to castigate poor Black males. There is little regard for their diminished voting power and political presence.

Even if a newly released offender with the "felon" label stamped on his forehead is lucky enough to land a job, Alexander details how he's often faced with insurmountable economic challenges. Up to 65 percent of his wages can be garnished to cover the child-support payments he missed while incarcerated. The remaining 35 percent could be garnished to go toward the payment of various fees, costs, and fines surrounding his confinement and probation. For example, an increasing number of states are requiring former prisoners to pay back court costs, processing fees, and the cost of legal representation related to their trials—even if they were assigned a public defender. Some are billed for the regular drug testing that may be required as a condition of their release.

These factors reinforce Alexander's charge that the criminal justice system is rigged to keep prison recidivism in constant motion. "About 70 percent of former prisoners are returned within three years," Alexander said during a 2002 interview with the radio show *Democracy Now!* "And the majority of those who are returned, are returned within three months, because the obstacles, the legal barriers to just surviving on the outside, are so great."

A capitalist society is fueled by materialism. There is no "off switch" for those born and raised in low-income communities. Bereft of common-sense community or culturally based means to generate income, many uneducated and uninspired youth turn to what they see in their communities as a perhaps dangerous but viable means to generate sources of income—drug sales. Unfortunately, you can't list "drug salesman" on your résumé.

As Michelle Alexander reminds us so persuasively, "What is completely missed in the rare public debates today about the plight of African Americans is that a huge percentage of them are not free to move up at all. It is not just that they lack opportunity, attend poor schools, or are plagued by poverty. They are barred by law from doing so . . . Young African American men now have criminal records and are thus subject to legalized discrimination for the rest of their lives . . . A human rights nightmare is occurring on our watch."

Dwayne, and kids like him, who turn to illegal ways to survive are absolutely wrong. But their desire to have the security that money promises is not only absolutely right, it's the American Dream.

Making Good on the Bounced Check

"Congress is fighting the wrong national deficit. The real deficit every leader needs to address is our human deficit and the immoral values that drive some extremist political leaders to hijack the nation's economic well-being and sacrifice the lives of innocent children and the poor."

Marian Wright Edelman used her August 19, 2011, column to speak for the 15.5 million children in America living in extreme poverty.

"As our nation pauses to honor Dr. Martin Luther King, Jr., with the dedication of a new memorial on the anniversary of the 1963 March on Washington," Edelman asked that we focus on a particular section of the "I Have a Dream" speech that King delivered during the historic occasion.

Dr. King, Edelman wrote, "reminded us that when our nation's founders wrote the Declaration of Independence and the Constitution, they had created a promissory note that guaranteed all Americans the inalienable rights of life, liberty, and the pursuit of happiness. But instead of honoring that promise for Black Americans, America had defaulted on it and given us a bad check that had come back marked 'insufficient funds.'"

When 42 percent of its children live in poverty, the country has indeed defaulted on its promise to help all Americans pursue life, liberty, and happiness. Those stunning figures were released in the August 2011 *Kids Count* report issued by the Baltimore-based Annie E. Casey Foundation. "The recession has basically wiped out any gains we made in the 1990s," said Patrick T. McCarthy, president of the foundation, who also addressed the country's dramatic increase in the child-poverty rate.

According to the report, children have been among the hardest hit by the nation's struggling economy, with the number living below the child-poverty rate (the threshold used by the study was a family of two adults and two children living on $43,512 a year) increasing by 18 percent between 2000 and 2009.

Eleven percent of the nation's children in 2010 had at least one unemployed parent, and, since 2011, 4 percent were affected by home foreclosures. Those numbers do not reflect families who were displaced in such instances as a landlord who lost or had to sell property they were renting.

Kids already under siege in low-income communities can expect even more challenges. The

Kids Count report, which has been issued annually for 20 years, also noted that during the country's four previous recessions, children trapped in the economic catastrophes were the ones most likely to exhibit behavioral problems, have difficulty in school, be less educated, earn less money, and have more health problems.

The March on Washington, Edelman reminded us, wasn't just about racial equality; it was about jobs and freedom and served as a massive people-driven "demand for economic opportunity and economic justice for all."

With a general election on the horizon and political leaders stubbornly entrenched in partisan deadlock, it's unlikely that improving the plight of African American boys will make the cut on most politicos' must-do lists.

What won't be should be.

A study prepared by Dr. Andrew Sum, director of the Center for Labor Market Studies at Northeastern University, found that opportunities are quickly vanishing for poorly educated, Black young people. In 2010 the unemployment, under-employment, and hidden unemployment rate for Black 16- to 29-year-olds was a jaw-dropping 40 percent. The large number of young Black adults *not* working full-time jobs, Sum's report noted, will drastically limit their future employability, earnings, and ability to support their families.

Edelman noted that there were 11 million poor children in America when Dr. King died. That number has quadrupled today. In a state of emergency, those on the lowest rungs of the social ladder suffer most. Black boys have been knocked off that ladder completely. This is not unfamiliar terrain for African Americans, who have a long and distinguished history of resilience and creative survival. In this crisis, we can ill afford to wait for someone else to save Black boys. The check has bounced, the dream . . . deferred. There is no cavalry on its way. If it's just us, so be it. We simply cannot, must not fail another generation of Black boys.

Rise of the Bonsai People

Jeff Henderson was living large in the mid-1980s. He was a shrewd and smooth drug dealer, swinging so much high-quality crack cocaine in South-Central Los Angeles that he cleared as much as $35,000 a week. At 19, Henderson was a millionaire running an extremely profitable business. He kept strict account of the cash flow and a keen eye on what went out and the multiplied sums that came back in. He was disciplined. Knowing it would dull his senses and make him easy prey, Henderson never used his product. He kept a cadre of well-rewarded soldiers who stayed in their boss's favor by executing quick, lucrative turnovers. Jeff worked hard to outsmart the competition, which was made up of rival drug dealers and cops anxious to bring his vibrant enterprise to an immediate halt.

Henderson had it all—lots of money, luxury cars, multiple houses, a bevy of beautiful ladies on demand, VIP access to all the high-end night spots and gambling joints. He was indeed living large.

Then, in 1988, he was busted and sent to prison for nine years.

Today, former drug dealer Jeff Henderson is better known nationwide as "Chef Jeff," celebrity cook, author of the *New York Times* best seller *Cooked: From the Streets to the Stove, from Cocaine to Foie Gras*, and former host of *The Chef Jeff Project* on the Food Network.

Henderson is a sought-after speaker on the lecture circuit. Prison saved his life, he tells audiences. It pulled him out of the fast lane and landed him in a place where he was forced to reevaluate the perilous path that led to a life of lockdown behind prison walls. "It's not anything I'm proud of. I'm socially conscious now; back then, I wasn't. My whole hustle revolved around desire for the finer things in life."

Henderson honed valuable skills on the streets that helped him survive and succeed in prison. With an oftentimes empty belly and a keen eye for opportunity, he noticed that the kitchen staff ate better than the other prisoners. He talked his way into the good graces of the prison officials, who allowed him to go from scrubbing pots and pans in the prison's kitchen to cooking with jailhouse chefs. He learned the intricacies of large-scale food production. Henderson also started drafting the manuscript for his book while he was still locked up. When he was released in 1996, the caged entrepreneur was ready to make his mark.

He'd read a newspaper article that featured influential Black chefs. Until reading the story, he hadn't realized there was such a thing as an "elite" Black chef. He sought out Robert Gadsby, a chef featured in the article and owner of a trendy Los Angeles restaurant. Henderson refused to take no for an answer. He needled Gadsby until the man agreed to give him an entry-level job as a dishwasher. The restaurateur would later say that Henderson's "tenacity and focus" reminded him of his younger self. Gadsby became the ex con's mentor, refining his rudimentary cooking skills and teaching him "kitchen culture."

Henderson has parlayed his street smarts and talent into celebrity.

"When you're born in poverty, the ability to survive is your daily bread. When you're a gang-banger or a drug dealer, you have to assess situations quickly and adapt outside your neighborhood or in another apartment complex because your life depends on it. You may change the color of your clothes, change your lingo and approach, and use your ability to play on people's psychological vulnerabilities and make them work to your advantage," Henderson explained. "It's the same way in the business world."

To emphasize his point, he drew an interesting analogy between drug sales and the housing market. Overseas drug lords would purposely dry up the market, making drug supplies virtually unavailable on the streets, he explained. Later, after demand was at a fever pitch, they'd flood the market and poor communities with higher-priced products. "It's like the housing market. Right now, hardly anyone's building new homes. You can get houses for next to nothing. But pretty soon, it will be a matter of more supply for newer, more expensive homes. That's when the real estate market will flip over again. It's the same concept with the drugs. There's a parallel; cocaine is a product, a revenue stream. It's supply and demand."

When he's sharing his story or participating in panel discussions, Henderson is quick to point out that he, like so many other young, disadvantaged Black men, was gifted the tools for success at birth. "I believe everybody is born with some sort of gifts—strengths and God-given talent. A lot of these hard-core gangbangers and drug dealers know about only what's in their environments. It's like living in a mental prison. But if you expose them outside of their worlds, it triggers inspiration for whatever they may be."

There are several benchmarks of Henderson's story that are crucial if it's to be used successfully as a model for reclaiming the lives and futures of Black boys. First, it must be recognized that Black boys, like all children, are born with the capacity to succeed. We just have to find ways to trigger the inspiration that Henderson talks about: "When I was in prison, I was exposed to the world of books. I hadn't experienced many things in life, but through books, I took mental journeys. I was able to see the world and myself differently."

Second, Black *men*—from ordinary to extraordinary—have got to be inspired and motivated to play important roles in the lives of wayward Black boys, even if they aren't related. Black men know the psychology, frustrations, desires, and needs of Black boys. Remember, it was a no-nonsense, street-savvy older Black man, Minister Baines, who was able to bust through the false bravado to help a kid by the name "Detroit Red" to discover Islam and his true purpose and potential as Malcolm X.

Similarly, Henderson was rescued by fellow prisoners. "There was a brother by the name of Kevin X, doing a 30-year sentence. He gave me my first book, *Black Men: Obsolete, Single, Dangerous?* by Haki Madhubuti. It was the first book I ever read," Henderson recalled. "In prison, I earned my Ph.D. in street-ology through books. Before then, I believed Jesus and God were white with blond hair and blue eyes; I believed I was inferior to white people. I never thought Black people had the ability to do anything great."

Henderson compared himself with a sponge, soaking up the information in the books that Kevin X and other prisoners shared with him. "When I began to read and study, I started questioning my thinking and actions. I understood why I hated myself, why I sold drugs, and why I was indirectly killing people who looked just like me," Henderson said. "I felt like I was robbed of this information in school," he added. "School never told me I have a rich history and Blacks made cultural contributions."

Muhammad Yunus, Nobel Prize–winning banker and author of the book *Creating a World Without Poverty*, often writes and speaks about the untapped potential of poor people:

> *To me poor people are like bonsai trees. When you plant the best seed of the tallest tree in a flower-pot, you get a replica of the tallest tree, only inches tall. There is nothing wrong with the seed you planted, only the soil-base that is too inadequate. Poor people are bonsai people. There is nothing wrong in their seeds. Simply, society never gave them the base to grow on.*

Beyond the much-needed intervention of public and private entities to stem the flow of Black boys from preschools to prisons, Black men can play vital roles, too. They don't need degrees or special pedigrees to use their passions and experience to fertilize the soil that will help Black boys grow into mighty trees.

When announcing the 2011 Town Hall meeting titled "The Disappearing Black Community and How We Get It Back: The Endangered Black Male," Syracuse University professor and founder of the Your Black World Coalition, Boyce Watkins, preached of a new, independent movement to save Black boys. "We need something that is no-nonsense and in your face," Watson said. "Many of the clowns in DC are not worth a nickel when it comes to our issues, because they've learned that there is nothing politically or economically profitable about supporting issues that affect the African American male.

"If we don't do it, then nobody else will."

SUMMONING THE WILL

Those who "will" confront a tremendous task. Black boys are removed from mainstream education in frighteningly large numbers through flawed disciplinary and intervention processes. Tragically, this institutionalized deficit spells out a dire fate for Black boys already facing disproportionate environmental burdens.

Perhaps some consolation can be taken from the fact that Black children overwhelmingly want positive change in their lives. For example, the Congressional Black Caucus's two-part series *Breaking Barriers: Plotting the Path to Academic Success for School-Age African-American Males* revealed that, among Black male juvenile detainees, 89.9 percent expressed a desire to return to school once they were released. More Black boys (45 percent) than white boys (36 percent) said they planned to attend college.

In January 2011, the Children's Defense Fund released the "Black Perspectives on What Black Children Face and What the Future Holds" research project as part of its Black Community Crusade for Children campaign, which was organized to confront the deepening crisis that Black children face. The research indicates a huge disconnect between adults and children when assessing the circumstances facing African Americans in the future, as well as perceptions of the problems and challenges Black communities are confronting in general.

Participants were asked, "How are things going in the country these days for Black children?" Sixty-nine percent of the adults said these are either "tough times" or "really bad times." Of the children asked the same question, 25 percent said "very good times," and the majority said these are "OK times."

In an attempt to gauge optimism, participants were asked to predict the climate for children in 15 years. Of all the adults, 54 percent said "things will be harder." Only 35 percent of the children agreed with that assessment.

Parents and children came closest to consensus on the question "What are the best things a parent or individual Black adult can do to help a Black child, make a positive difference?"

Thirty-one percent of the adults and 25 percent of the children agree that talking to youth, being involved, spending time, and communicating were the best ways to make a positive impact on youth. The percentages were similar on other suggestions such as instill good moral values; parents letting children know they care; being good role models; and being available to assist, support, and listen to children.

Both the Congressional Black Caucus and the Children's Defense Fund studies reveal that adults and children want the same thing. Although the degrees of optimism may vary, both groups believe in education and active parental involvement, and want to live in places where children can survive and thrive.

Tavis Smiley plans to use his resources to help in that process. "While working on the television special, I came face-to-face with Black boys trapped in a dysfunctional and broken educational system. I spent hours with brave and innovative educators determined to make a difference," Smiley explained. "When the interviews were over and the cameras stopped rolling, I was determined to make sure that I personally, and the Tavis Smiley Foundation, did our part."

Vonda Paige, the executive director of the Tavis Smiley Foundation, described the reasons the Foundation is involved and the role it will play: "Given what we know about the challenges and barriers to learning, it really will take the whole village to educate our children for the future. And we must start with our support and education of parents.

"There is overwhelming research that recognizes that parents are a child's best first teacher and play critical roles in determining their child's academic performance," Paige said. With this critical information in mind, the Tavis Smiley Foundation rolled out the Too Important to Fail national educational initiative in September. This effort, which includes Parent Summits, a reading mobile truck tour, and an interactive Web site (www.tooimportanttofail.com), was launched to inform and empower parents and communities. By sharing the latest information, research, programs, family and school partnership material, as well as other valuable resources, the Foundation is demonstrating its commitment to building a cadre of advocates for the development of children. The cross-country seminars and truck tour will take these endeavors on the road. Sessions will teach, explain, and share parent in-home literacy and homework strategies; state and federal legislation; how parents with special-needs children can access local and state resources; and grade-level readiness material that parents can use to help their child read at grade level.

WHATEVER WE CAN, WHATEVER WE HAVE, WHEREVER WE ARE

Three hundred miles south of Alameda County, the Los Angeles Conservation Corps has taken a unique approach with young Black male high school dropouts. If the boys go back and work to get their high school diplomas, the conservation corps gives them a job while they're doing it.

Walter Finnie, a tenth grader at Domingus High in Compton, accepted that deal. He was about to drop out when a friend told him about the conservation corps and how it would be good for him as he worked his way through school. During his interview, Walter, wearing his green plastic hat and safety goggles, explained how the program works and its impact on his life. "What we do is, every day after lunch, Karen picks us up in the van and we'll go ride around the streets of L.A., and we'll clean alleys and, you know, clean lots . . . spruce up the city.

"When I'm cleaning alleys, I'm thinking, like, I really don't like doing this," Walter laughed. "But it's for the better of me. It's experience. I just feel like no matter what it is I have to do, I'm gonna do it. This is a great opportunity to help me grow as a young man, especially where I'm growing up—the environment around—this keeps me out of the dangers. So, you know."

The Los Angeles Conservation Corps offers a common-sense, unique approach that helps Black boys avoid the distractions of the streets while earning a little money and staying in school.

Yet considering the number of Black boys who drop out of school and wind up pursuing fleeting and dangerous careers in the drug trade, there is a need for many more grassroots approaches, where boys and disadvantaged students can earn spending money, stay on steady paths at school, and avoid the seduction of the streets.

Marian Wright Edelman's evolutionary education project, the Freedom School Program, has been spreading across the country since 1995. Rooted in the educational work during the Civil Rights Movement, the schools engage children (grades K–12) during a six to seven week summer program. The program targets the "learning loss" that they typically experience when school is not in session. There are five essential components of the Freedom School Programs: high-quality academic enrichment; parent and family involvement; social action and civic engagement; intergenerational servant leadership development; and nutrition, health, and mental health.

Since its inception, more than 70,000 children and families have benefited from the Children's Defense Fund's Freedom Schools' experience. Additionally, more than 7,000 college students and 1,500 adults have been trained to teach the program. The Freedom Schools served nearly 9,000 children at 142 sites in 75 cities during the summer of 2011.

The key to the program's success is its partnerships with community-based organizations, faith institutions, municipalities, schools, colleges, and universities. Imagine how many more Black boys in low-income areas could be served if more churches, other Black agencies, and motivated individuals made commitments to develop CDF Freedom Schools in their neighborhoods.

Al Dotson, Jr., chairman of 100 Black Men of America, challenged his group during the organization's 23rd annual convention: "There is an enormous achievement and opportunity gap impacting African American youth as it relates to grade-level education and higher-education opportunities. This year's record-setting conference tackled these issues from a global perspective, finding solutions to educating our young men and women and directing our members to act and inspire others to act on the solutions discussed."

Education Secretary Arne Duncan praised and endorsed the organization's clarion call to action, for good reasons: "This is why I am such a big fan of what the 100 Black Men are doing . . . when our children have the opportunity to be surrounded by adults who care passionately about them and stick with them for the long haul, they will do fantastic."

Organizations are playing valuable roles in efforts to stem the crisis. However, with more than a million kids failing to complete high school—with Black boys representing the bulk of that number—an all-hands-on-deck approach is necessary. This means that we can't rely on organizations and institutions alone. To even begin to turn the tide of this battle, individuals must also bring their will, energy, and creativity to the front lines.

Nell Noddings, a professor at Stanford University, a former K–12 math teacher, and the author of several books on the ethics of care and education, spoke to the need for caring Black mentors to lovingly intervene in the lives of troubled

Black boys: "Many studies show the single most important thing in turning lives around is the ongoing presence of a caring adult. Young Black men and boys growing up without male role models and in conditions of poverty probably do need, more than anyone else, that assurance that somebody really cares."

THE WAR OF ONE

Ultimately, "love" was the weapon that won the battle for civil rights. People—regular, ordinary individuals—joined together; disobeyed unrighteous authority figures; withstood batons and skin-shredding fire hoses; risked their lives; and fought with ballots, boots, broken bones, and sheer will until America's version of apartheid succumbed to the love of humanity.

The system that's failing Black boys and low-income students wasn't broken in a vacuum. The forces of poverty, racism, crime, unemployment, missing fathers, and distracted and overworked mothers exacerbate a monumental problem.

Love in the form of individual and community action is needed in the movement to bring justice and humanity to long-neglected or ignored minority children and Black boys.

Individuals—mothers, fathers, neighbors, preachers, business owners, and activists—must also suit up for battle. Here too there are brave soldiers in the arena doing their best to rescue and reclaim endangered Black boys.

C3: CARING, CONNECTING, AND COMMITTING

No one disputes the level of crisis in our public schools. We confront a tsunami of challenges that threatens to leave Black boys in its wake, with no real hope and no real future other than a lifetime of incarceration.

Are we just to sit back and watch the destructive waves?

Are we simply to write off another generation of Black boys because they are just that—Black boys: misunderstood, maligned, and marked for failure?

Are we to swap promise for prisons, incarceration for investment in young, untapped human potential?

No! A hundred times, No!

A promise is inscribed in the United States Declaration of Independence, and we must not allow this country to renege on its pledge. Poet extraordinaire Langston Hughes framed our collective responsibility this way:

> O, yes, I say it plain, America never was America to me. And yet, I swear this oath— America will be!

America *will be* a place where the most vulnerable will also receive the necessary attention and resources to survive and thrive both in this country and abroad. America *will be* a place where a multitiered discriminatory educational system that disseminates education according to class, race, and location is no longer tolerated.

How is this sea change in attitudes and action supposed to take place?

You, me, us, we! The damning research, statistics, predictions, and dire outcomes serve as our call to action. The engines that drive our contributions can be summed up with three words of action: *caring, connecting,* and *committing.*

When we unpack the three C's, we better understand our roles:

Caring: We have to challenge ourselves to see ourselves in these boys. When we care, we no longer see statistics, stereotypes, or dismissible demographics—we see human beings. Black boys, welcomed into the arc of brotherhood, can no longer be the scapegoats for all of our fears.

We respond to issues we care about. When we care, Black boys are no longer considered the "other," or society's outcasts. Because we care we can challenge institutions that treat boys as budgetary casualties.

Caring does not permit us to throw money at a problem, then walk away feeling vindicated. We involve ourselves in implementation. We ask about outcomes and demand results. We help move the needle, with the knowledge that it can't move without hands-on involvement.

When we care, we meet eye to eye, shake hands, hug, and hold those in desperate need of loving care.

Caring moves us to *connect*:

When we connect, we call, go for walks together, sit in classrooms, talk to teachers, visit homes, meet parents. We talk, and more important, we listen.

Connecting means we link our lives to a Black boy's life. They need one-on-one interaction with caring adults, especially caring adult Black males. We connect bodies with need. Connecting means placing adults in the lives of fatherless boys. If we are African American males, we connect our faces, stories, values, jobs, hardships, and triumphs to their worlds. If we are not, perhaps we ask a Black male friend or colleague to join us to add the much-needed cultural piece to the other layers we've provided to help a Black boy navigate real life.

We also connect resources to those who need them—teachers, counselors, and parents. If books are needed at a school, grassroots agency, or local juvenile center, we make sure they are purchased and delivered. If a Black boy needs a trusted person to read to him, we make sure we or someone we know is available. Connecting means showing up at schools with our sleeves rolled up, ready to move our passions into action.

After we *connect*, it is imperative that we *commit*.

Commitment means "no retreat"; we're in it for the long haul. When we are committed, the stumbles and falls, perceived failures and setbacks, and sometimes outright rebellion do not deter us. Commitment means that we take responsibility for the success or failure of children.

Commitment means consistency; we are not drive-by surrogates. We understand the challenges and seek solutions. We go outside our personal prisms and vow to keep preconceptions, prejudices, and biases at a distance.

Through our commitments to time and space, a child learns trust, discipline, and respect for other human beings.

The crisis confronting Black boys demands a C3 approach. It requires each of us to examine our gifts, our strengths, our networks, and our affiliations and to ask one probing but important question:

"What can I do right now?"

We know there are no easy fixes, no quick roads to solutions. We know teachers need parental support, new recruits, access to the latest research and professional development, and, in many instances, better pay.

Teachers need a team of community supporters who will help them wrestle with the massive social and economic challenges that, through no fault of their own, enter their classrooms on the faces of the children they teach.

This journey has convinced us that test scores cannot be deemed the ultimate measure of Black boys' worth. Surely we can develop a unique and valid system that does not overlook humanity for the sake of efficiency.

It is a simple fact that bears repeating: Black boys need to see themselves in our country's narrative and in their school hallways. If we can't accomplish this task, school simply won't make sense to them.

Perhaps the most important lesson we've gleaned from interviewing, filming, listening to, and writing about these boys is that each and every one needs and deserves at least one adult in his life—an adult who watches over him like a hawk and stubbornly refuses to let him fail.

When boys have *even that one* vigilant adult, they succeed.

If we employ the C3, "caring, connecting, and committing," it can happen.

In this case, we should dispense with the word "if." It must be . . . "if America is to be."

Simply put, we have no options.

Our children, especially our Black boys under siege, are *too important to fail!*

RESOURCE GUIDE

Too Important
to Fail
Resource Guide

Dear Reader,

Now that you've had a chance to read the first section of the book, perhaps you have discovered new perspectives—both enlightening and challenging—about the state of your educational system, your local schools, and perhaps even your own home. We hope the facts have motivated you to take the message of this book to heart and to become part of the solution. Undoubtedly you must have many questions about what you can do as an individual, a single parent, a group of teachers, or just a concerned citizen. What follows is a reference guide to help you get started.

Here you will find information related to the physical, psychological and educational well-being of African American boys and children in need. You will find agencies and organizations created to increase and improve retention and graduation rates, as well as mentoring and role model networks and services that parents, educators, and communities alike need in order to help our children succeed. Our reading list contains research and data that present a clearer picture of the challenges that impede and opportunities that improve the way our children learn.

We urge you to keep an open mind exploring these resources. If you're a parent, you may want to immediately check out the PARENTAL SUPPORT or AFTER SCHOOL categories to see if any of the programs or organizations are in your area. If you're a teacher or educator, you may want to peruse the MENTORING and TEACHER/EDUCATOR TRAINING sections to learn how you can better provide for your children and community. We encourage everyone to read the entries carefully and consider how every program or organization might be of assistance to you and your community.

We present this material to you in the fervent hope that it will help your child succeed. We invite you to explore this material and explore it often. Consider it your go-to source to plan better, fight harder, and ultimately be a part of an urgent movement that refuses to let Black boys or any child in need fail.

How to Use the Resource Guide:

The following index provides an easy to access reference list of 130 sources categorized by who and what they are and how they can help you. All 130 entries have been numbered and categorized by their primary mission. Organizations that offer multiple services may be listed under more than one category.

To use this guide, simply choose the category of interest to you. The numbers beneath each category correspond to the organizations numbered and listed alphabetically in the following pages. For example, under "MENTORING," # 1 refers to the organization 100 Black Men; under "JUVENILE JUSTICE," #61 refers to the organization Models for Change. Listed organizations also have Web site addresses and phone numbers for contact.

ADVOCACY
4, 10, 19, 23, 33, 46, 63, 64, 65, 66, 67, 68, 71, 81, 88, 91, 92, 102, 107, 111, 114

AFTER SCHOOL AND ACADEMIC ENRICHMENT PROGRAMS
2, 3, 6, 7, 11, 16, 17, 18, 24, 28, 29, 38, 39, 42, 53, 55, 67, 70, 76, 82, 93, 105, 106, 107, 116, 123, 124, 130

CAREER BUILDING
29, 35, 37, 50, 51, 52, 54, 82, 96, 123, 129, 130

COLLEGE PREP
27, 28, 32, 35, 40, 44, 50, 51

EARLY CHILDHOOD
23, 26, 36, 47, 53, 91, 92, 120, 128

HEALTH AND WELL-BEING
5, 6, 15, 63, 91, 121, 124, 125

JUVENILE JUSTICE
19, 33, 42, 61, 63, 75, 79, 80, 94, 98, 107, 108, 111, 115

MENTORING
1, 6, 9, 11, 17, 25, 30, 34, 38, 39, 42, 48, 53, 57, 59, 60, 107, 113, 126

PARENTAL SUPPORT
7, 12, 32, 39, 53, 58, 65, 68, 70, 73, 74, 75, 89, 90, 99, 100, 102, 103, 104, 105, 106, 124

RESEARCH & POLICY
1, 15, 19, 20, 21, 23, 28, 33, 47, 56, 66, 69, 71, 81, 85, 101, 107, 109, 110, 114, 115, 117, 119, 121

TEACHER/EDUCATOR TRAINING
25, 43, 45, 46, 47, 66, 72, 74, 78, 83, 84, 85, 90, 97, 99, 107, 112, 114, 122

YOUTH DEVELOPMENT
4, 7, 8, 13, 14, 16, 17, 18, 24, 25, 26, 31, 35, 39, 49, 52, 53, 55, 56, 62, 67, 71, 76, 80, 81, 83, 86, 87, 88, 96, 107, 113, 118, 125, 127, 128, 129, 130

1. 100 BLACK MEN OF AMERICA, INC.

100 Black Men of America, Inc. seeks to serve as a beacon of leadership by utilizing diverse talents to create environments where children are motivated to achieve, and to empower African Americans to become self-sufficient shareholders in the economic and social fabric of the communities it serves. 100 Black Men of America, Inc. is committed to the intellectual development of youth and the economic empowerment of the African American community based on the following precepts: respect for family, spirituality, justice, and integrity. Through a worldwide network of chapters Mentoring the 100 Way® is a holistic mentoring program that addresses the social, emotional, and cultural needs of children ages 8–18. Members of the 100 are trained and certified to become mentors, advocates, and role models for the youth within their communities.

Web site: www.100blackmen.org

Phone: (404) 688-5100

2. AFTER-SCHOOL ALL-STARS

After-School All-Stars provides free comprehensive after-school programs to nearly 81,000 children in need on over 450 school sites in 12 different cities from NYC to Hawaii. Their programs incorporate academic support, enrichment opportunities, and health & fitness activities. ASAS offers after-school programs for tutoring at-risk youth and essential support to middle-school-aged kids.

Web site: www.afterschoolallstars.org

Phone: (310) 275-3232

3.   AL WOOTEN JR. HERITAGE CENTER

The Al Wooten Jr. Heritage Center provides a safe and nurturing environment where boys and girls ages 8–18 can participate in academic enrichment programs and recreational activities exploring a world of opportunities. The Center is a neighborhood approach to the revitalization and empowerment of a community in crisis. They provide a safe and nurturing environment and are committed to good citizenship and academic excellence. Resources include a college preparatory track provided by College Track, a tutorial program, a private computer lab, the Ella Fitzgerald Library, homework assistance, and a 16-week violence prevention program called Street Soldiers.

Web site: www.wootencenter.org

Phone: (323) 756-7203

4. AMERICA'S PROMISE—THE ALLIANCE FOR YOUTH

Founded in 1997 with General Colin Powell as Chairman and chaired today by Alma Powell, America's Promise Alliance is a cross-sector partnership of 400+ corporations, nonprofits, faith-based organizations, and advocacy groups that are passionate about improving lives and changing outcomes for children. A top priority of the organization is ensuring that all young people graduate from high school ready for college, work, and life. The work of this organization involves raising awareness, encouraging action, and engaging in advocacy to provide children the key supports they call the Five Promises: Caring Adults, Safe Places, A Healthy Start, An Effective Education, and Opportunities to Help Others.

Web site: www.americaspromise.org

Phone: (202) 657-0600

5. ASSOCIATION OF BLACK PSYCHOLOGISTS

The Association of Black Psychologists is dedicated to creating a positive impact on the mental health of the national Black community by means of planning, programs, services, training, and advocacy. Current programs and initiatives are designed to: enhance the psychological well-being of Black people in America; promote positive approaches to research; develop an approach to psychology consistent with the experience of Black people; define mental health in consonance with newly established psychological concepts and standards regarding Black people; develop policies for local, state and national decision-making that impact the mental health of the Black community; and promote values and a lifestyle that support our survival and well-being as a race.

Web site: www.abpsi.org

Phone: (202) 722-0808

6.   ATHLETES AGAINST DRUGS

AAD's mission is to leverage national and local athletes, celebrities, and corporate leaders to inspire, educate, and help youth make healthy life decisions. They desire to help youth develop life skills and prepare them for economic opportunities that will change their lives. The AAD Literacy Program promotes and increases literacy among youth, particularly those reading two to three years below grade level. The ultimate goal is empowering students to become avid readers, positively impacting their overall academic performance. AAD's Mentor Program connects youth with real world environmental duties and provides them with a forum to explore issues such as goal setting, higher education, and career options.

Web site: www.athletesagainstdrugs.com

Phone: (312) 321-3400

7.   BETTER FAMILY LIFE, INC.

Better Family Life, Inc. (BFL) is a nonprofit corporation dedicated to the prosperity and growth of the American family. It is committed to finding internal solutions to the crises within the African American family; BFL offers social, cultural, artistic, youth, economic, housing, and educational programs that help to promote positive and innovative changes within the metropolitan St. Louis area. Geared towards disadvantaged and skill-deficient youth, BFL has spent two decades offering a full spectrum of programs including after-school, in-school and summer programs, cultural youth programs and family support services.

Web site: http://www.betterfamilylife.org/

Phone: (314) 367-3440

8.   BEYOND THE BRICKS PROJECT

Beyond the Bricks: A New Era in Education is a documentary film that serves as the foundation for a community-based movement and online network that promotes solutions for the consistently low performance of African American boys in the public school system. The film follows African American students Shaquiel Ingram and Erick Graham as they struggle to stay on track in the Newark, NJ, public school system. In danger of becoming just another couple of statistics on the "school-to-prison pipeline," the boys find a lifeline with support from compassionate community leaders and alternative education programs that address the root causes of their problems. Woven into the boys' stories is commentary from some of the country's foremost scholars and experts focused on African American boys and their education.

Web site: www.beyondthebricksproject.com

Phone: (212) 234-3925

9.   BIG BROTHERS BIG SISTERS

As the nation's largest donor-and-volunteer-supported mentoring network, Big Brothers Big Sisters makes meaningful, monitored matches between adult volunteers ("Bigs") and children ("Littles"), ages 6 through 18, in communities across the country. BBBS develops positive relationships that have a direct and lasting effect on the lives of young people. By partnering with parents/guardians, volunteers, and others in the community, BBBS is accountable for each child in their program achieving: higher aspirations, greater confidence, better relationships, avoidance of risky behaviors, and educational success.

Web site: www.bbbs.org

Phone: (215) 567-7000

10. BLACK ALLIANCE FOR EDUCATIONAL OPTIONS (BAEO)

BAEO is one of the preeminent national organizations for African Americans who support educational options. Through its local chapters and national initiatives it is devoted to increased access to high-quality educational options for Black children by actively supporting parental choice policies and programs that empower low-income and working-class Black families. BAEO firmly believes parental choice programs, which lead to the creation of quality educational options, will not only rescue children, but create powerful incentives for all schools, public and private, to improve.

Web site: www.baeo.org

Phone: (202) 429-2236

11.   BLACK MALE INITIATIVE PROGRAM

The Black Male Initiative Program (BMI), endeavors to increase and improve retention and graduation rates for Black males. Their academic, community outreach, and mentoring activities are designed to aid Black males in their quest for a college degree. BMI is engaged in establishing academic study groups, mentor-mentee relationship-building, career awareness activities, and progressive leadership programming.

Web site: www.theblackmaleinitiative.org
Phone: (301) 314-7760, or (301) 314-8439

12.   BLACK PARENT NETWORK

This online organization provides a Web site portal designed to support Black parents, parents, caregivers, and professionals by providing them with information about a wide range of parenting issues. Registered members can have free access to the site and participate as a community member through the notice board to exchange ideas and get support from other parents.

Web site: www.blackparentnetwork.com/
Phone: (612) 568-6326 or (877) 378-4326

13. BOY SCOUTS OF AMERICA

The Boy Scouts of America is one of the nation's largest and most prominent values-based youth development organizations. The BSA provides a program for young people that builds character, trains them in the responsibilities of participating citizenship, and develops personal fitness.

The Boy Scouts of America believes—and, through over a century of experience, knows—that helping youth is a key to building a more conscientious, responsible, and productive society.

Web site: www.scouting.org

Phone: (972) 580-2000

14. BOYS AND GIRLS CLUBS OF AMERICA

The mission of the Boys and Girls Clubs of America is to enable all young people, especially those who are in need, to reach their full potential as productive, caring, responsible citizens. Their core beliefs are that their clubs provide: a safe place to learn and grow; ongoing relationships with caring, adult professionals; life-enhancing programs and character-development experiences; hope; and opportunity. The Boys and Girls

Clubs of America have taken a major advocacy position on the high school dropout crisis. See the BGCA position paper "Our Nation's Dropout Crisis is Everyone's Problem."

Web site: www.bgca.org

Phone: (404) 487-5700

15.   BOYS AND YOUNG MEN OF COLOR (BMOC)

The Boys and Young Men of Color project sponsored by the Chief Justice Earl Warren Institute on Race, Ethnicity and Diversity, and the California Endowment is the nation's first research and policy symposium focused on the well-being of boys and young men of color. It presents leading research and resources for policy advocates and activists focused on these important issues.

The project brings together university-based scholars, community-based leaders, and public policy makers to consider integrated/inter-segmental approaches to improving the life chances of young Black and Latino men in four areas: Education, Health, Community Services, and the Built Environment. The BMOC's first publication, *Changing Places: How Communities Will Improve the Health of Boys of Color*, provides a road map of evidence-based intervention strategies for policy-makers, local leaders, and agencies.

Web site: www.boysandmenofcolor.org

Phone: (866) 833-3533

16. Boys Club of New York

BCNY has helped thousands of boys develop into quality young men. They have focused on character development, academic achievement, nourishing creativity, developing social skills, physical fitness, and athletic participation. At BCNY their focus is on the most significant positive outcome they can work toward: helping at-risk boys of New York City grow up into mature, successful young men. They make a commitment to every boy who joins BCNY that they will work tirelessly to provide him with the skills, confidence, and discipline that will enable him to reach for the sky and achieve his full potential.

Web site: www.bcny.org

Phone: (212) 677-1102

17. Building Educated Leaders for Life (BELL)

BELL is a leading nonprofit provider of research-based, educational summer and after-school experiences for children in grades K–8. It works to ensure all children have the learning opportunities they need to fulfill their potential in school and in life. Research shows that a lack of additional learning time—and in particular, a lack of summer learning opportunities—causes up to two-thirds of the academic achievement gap between children from low-income communities and their higher-income peers. BELL exists to transform the academic achievements, self-confidence, and life trajectories of children living in under-resourced, urban communities. BELL gives students the benefit of small-group academic instruction, mentorship, a wide range of enrichment activities, and community engagement.

Web site: www.bellnational.org

Phone: (617) 282-1567

18. CAMP FIRE USA

Camp Fire USA's mission is to build caring, confident youth and future leaders. Camp Fire's programs contribute to the community by engaging youth in educational, enrichment, and service-learning programs that address social issues and build life skills. It connects children with caring, trained adults in a small-group atmosphere, while also connecting families with each other in their communities. It does this by offering age-appropriate youth, teen, and family clubs. Camp Fire offers early childhood, before-and-after-school, full-day, school-break and drop-in center programs supporting the child care needs of families. Children participate in indoor and outdoor age-appropriate small-group activities where they can explore personal interests, learn to make healthy choices, develop social skills, and have fun.

Web site: www.campfireusa.org

Phone: (816) 285-2010

19. CAMPAIGN FOR BLACK MALE ACHIEVEMENT

George Soros's Open Society Foundation's Campaign for Black Male Achievement is a multi-issue, cross-fund strategy that aims to address Black men and boys' exclusion from economic, social, educational, and political life in the United States. The campaign responds to a growing body of research that reveals the intensification of Black males' negative life outcomes. The Foundation funds scholarly work that seeks to reduce in-carceration, promote racial justice, and support youth engagement and leadership development. Recognizing that policies that perpetuate Black male exclusion are state- and locally-based, the campaign has adopted a "place-based" grant-making approach that provides investments in specific geographic regions, including the Midwest, with a focus on Chicago, Illinois, and Milwaukee, Wisconsin; the Gulf Region, with a focus on New Orleans, Louisiana, and Jackson, Mississippi; and the Mid-Atlantic, with a focus on Baltimore, Maryland, and Philadelphia, Pennsylvania.

Web site: www.soros.org/cbma

Phone: (212) 548-0132

20. CENTER FOR AFRICAN AMERICAN RESEARCH AND POLICY

The Center for African American Research and Policy (CAARP) relies on scholarly research to advance critical discourse and promote informed decisions as it pertains to policy issues confronting African Americans in both the academic setting and society at large. The breadth and depth of research and policy-oriented projects encompasses the full tapestry of the "African American Predicament" and reflects the wide diversity of academic backgrounds of the affiliated researchers at the Center.

Web site: caarpweb.com

Phone: (866) 580-7979

21. CENTER FOR LAW AND SOCIAL POLICY (CLASP)

CLASP works to promote policies that support both child development and the needs of low-income working parents. It believes that high-quality child care and early education builds a strong foundation for young children's healthy development and ensures that they have what's needed to thrive.

Through careful research and analysis and effective advocacy, CLASP develops and promotes new ideas, mobilizes others, and directly assists governments and advocates putting in place successful strategies that deliver results that matter to people across America. It supports policies that expand resources for child care and early education at the federal, state, and local levels. CLASP studies the relationships between the child care subsidy systems, Head Start and Early Head Start, state pre-kindergarten programs, and other birth-to-five early education efforts, to advance ideas that address the full range children and family needs.

Web site: www.clasp.org

Phone: (202) 906-8000

22. **CENTER FOR NEIGHBORHOOD ENTERPRISE**

The Center for Neighborhood Enterprise helps residents of low-income neighborhoods address the problems of their communities. It strives to transform lives, schools, and troubled neighborhoods from the inside out. CNE's grassroots network addresses: youth-violence, substance abuse, teen pregnancy, homelessness, joblessness, family dissolution, poor education, and deteriorating neighborhoods. Because civil order is fundamental to economic revitalization, CNE has a major focus on youth violence intervention and prevention. The Center's Violence-Free Zone initiative, with VFZ sites in Baltimore; Chicago; Dallas; Milwaukee; and Richmond, VA, is significantly reducing youth violence in high-risk middle and high schools nationwide. CNE also provides effective community and faith-based organizations with training and technical assistance, links them to sources of support, and evaluates their experiences for public policy.

Web site: www.cneonline.org

Phone: (202) 518-6500

23.   CHILDREN'S DEFENSE FUND

From its inception in 1973, the Children's Defense Fund has challenged the United States to raise its standards by improving policies and programs for children. It is known for outstanding research on children's survival, protection, and development in all racial and income groups, and for independent analyses of federal and state policies that affect children, families and communities. CDF provides a strong, effective, and independent voice for all the children of America who cannot vote, lobby, or speak for themselves. It focuses particular attention on the needs of poor and minority children and those with disabilities. CDF educates the nation about the needs of children and encourages preventive investments before they get sick, drop out of school, get into trouble, or suffer family breakdown. The CDF's Leave No Child Behind® mission insures every child has "a Healthy Start, a Head Start, a Fair Start, a Safe Start, a Moral Start in life" and "successful passage to adulthood with the help of caring families and communities."

Web site: www.childrensdefense.org

Phone: (800) CDF-1200 [(800) 233-1200]

24.   CITIZEN SCHOOLS

Citizen Schools partners with middle schools to expand the learning day for children in low-income communities across the country. Using Expanded Learning Time (ELT) it works to close the achievement gap and enable successful transitions into high school and increase graduation rates. Citizen Schools states that by increasing the school day by 30 to 60 percent, schools will have the opportunity to provide students with the time, enrichment, and instruction they need to meet today's high academic standards. Schools that adopt Expanded Learning Time significantly extend their schedules for all students by lengthening the school day, school year, or both.

Web site: www.citizenschools.org

Phone: (617) 695-2300

25.   CITY YEAR

City Year is a "citizen service movement" that unites young people of all backgrounds for a year of full-time service, giving them the skills and opportunities to change the world. With locations across the United States, "corps members" serve for 10 months, putting their idealism to work for children and communities through school-based service, youth leadership programs, and community transformation. City Year's youth service corps is one of the largest in America, with initiatives tailored to meet community and school district needs. Corps members serve in schools as tutors, mentors, role models, and leaders of after-school programs. They help improve student attendance, behavior, and coursework—which increases the possibilities of their graduating high school. This school-based service is at the heart of City Year's "Whole School, Whole Child" approach to helping students and schools succeed.

Web site: www.cityyear.org

Phone: (617) 927-2500

26.   COALITION FOR COMMUNITY SCHOOLS

The Coalition for Community Schools, housed at the Institute for Educational Leadership, is an alliance of national, state, and local organizations in education K–16, youth development, community planning and development, family support, health and human services, government, and philanthropy, as well as national, state, and local community school networks.

The Early Childhood and Community Schools Linkages Project demonstrates strategic linkages between quality comprehensive early childhood opportunities and effective community schools that lead to better results and future educational success for vulnerable children. The Linkage Project focuses on several key indicators: parent involvement, early chronic absenteeism, and reading by the third grade. The Community Schools Web site shares the Project's research with other communities to inform, influence, and inspire the development of a common state legislative framework that supports educational reform.

Web site: www.communityschools.org

Phone: (202) 822-8405, ext 156

27. COLLEGE SUMMIT

College Summit is a national nonprofit organization that partners with schools and districts to strengthen college-going culture and increases college enrollment rates, so that all high school students graduate career- and-college-ready. College Summit arms students with the resources and information that's necessary when applying to college, such as test prep courses, college visits, and application guidance. Through innovative partnerships, College Summit provides educators and students with the right tools, resources, and experiences to better navigate the difficult transition from grade 12 to grade 13.

Web site: www.collegesummit.org

Phone: (202) 319-1763

28. COMMUNITIES IN SCHOOLS

Communities In Schools is a nationwide network of passionate professionals working in public schools to surround students with a community of support, empowering them to stay in school and achieve in life. Their nearly 200 local affiliates serve the lowest performing schools and the students most likely to drop out of high school. Their network is composed of nearly 5,000 passionate professionals in 25 states and the District of Columbia. The agency serves nearly 1.3 million young people in more than 3,400 schools. CIS is actively engaged with policy makers, school administrators, parents, and business partners to ensure that its services are extended to as many K–12 students as possible and that those students have access to college.

Web site: www.communitiesinschools.org

Phone: (703) 519-8999

29. COMPUTER CLUBHOUSE

The Computer Clubhouse provides a creative and safe out-of-school learning environment where young people from underserved communities work with adult mentors to explore their own ideas, develop skills, and build confidence in themselves through the use of technology. Using the "original" Clubhouse as a model, the Computer Clubhouse Network supports community-based Clubhouses around the world, providing over 25,000 youth per year with access to resources, skills, and experiences to help them succeed in their careers, contribute to their communities, and lead outstanding lives. The Clubhouse learning approach, grounded in research from the fields of education, developmental and social psychology, cognitive science, and youth development, is designed to empower youth from all backgrounds to become more capable, creative, and confident learners.

Web site: www.computerclubhouse.org

Phone: (617) 589-0271

30. Concerned Black Men

Concerned Black Men (CBM) has been committed to filling the void of positive Black male role models in many communities for over 30 years. It provides mentors and programs that youth need, while providing opportunities for academic and career enrichment.

The CBM CARES® National Mentoring Initiative provides middle school boys with responsible and caring adult male mentors. The Young Males of Color Cross Cities Collaborative (YMC3) is a newly designed CBM program focusing on young Black males in Baltimore, Philadelphia, and Washington, DC. YMC3's goal is to improve the lives of young males of color in the areas of achievement, college, and careers.

Web site: www.cbmnational.org

Phone: (202) 783-6119, Toll Free: (888) 395-7816

31. **CORPORATION FOR NATIONAL AND COMMUNITY SERVICE**

The Corporation for National and Community Service is a federal agency that engages more than 5 million Americans in service through Senior Corps, AmeriCorps, Learn and Serve America, Foster Grandparents Program, and the Retired and Senior Volunteer Program. It also provides the "Community Guide to Helping America's Youth," a Web-based tool with up-to-date research on youth development and effective programs. The CNCS leads President Obama's national call to service initiative, "United We Serve." Over 62.8 million adults served almost 8.1 billion hours through organizations in 2010.

Web site: www.nationalservice.gov

Phone: (202) 606-5000

32. COUNCIL OF AFRICAN AMERICAN PARENTS (CAAP)

CAAP is a college preparatory program rooted in academics, testing prep, study skills, cultural enrichment, self-awareness and confidence building from 6th through 12th grade. CAAP students begin taking the SAT as early as 11 years of age.

CAAP is designed to empower and equip parents with tools and resources that will help maximize their child's learning potential and increase their academic performance. The single most important thing that parents and community members can do for our children is to ensure that they will be prepared: to compete for seats at selective colleges and universities, become productive and responsible leaders, and make positive contributions to our families, communities, and society at large.

Web site: www.councilofafricanamerican
parents.org/resources.html

Phone: (909) 263-2354

33. CRADLE TO PRISON PIPELINE CAMPAIGN

The Children's Defense Fund's Cradle to Prison Pipeline® Campaign is committed to dismantling that pipeline, however long it takes. It focuses first on preventing children from entering the juvenile justice system.

Secondly, it helps kids already trapped in the pipeline find a way out, liberating them from the lifelong spiral of arrest and incarceration.

CDF's Cradle to Prison Pipeline® Campaign is designed to reduce detention and incarceration by increasing preventive supports and services children need, such as access to quality early childhood development and education services, and accessible, comprehensive health and mental health coverage.

Web site: www.childrensdefense.
org/programs-campaigns/
cradle-to-prison-pipeline

Phone: (800) 233-1200

34. CREATIVE MENTORING

Creative Mentoring®, a program of Connecting Generations, supports in-school mentoring programs in New Castle, Kent, and Sussex Counties of Delaware. It provides quality training to volunteer in-school mentors and helps schools design and implement quality in-school mentoring programs. Creative Mentors help children—through personal, one-on-one time in schools once a week—develop their unique qualities and reach their full potential.

Web site: www.connecting-generations.org

Phone: (302) 656-2122

35. DIGIT ALL SYSTEMS, INC.

Digit All Systems, Inc. is a 501(c) (3) nonprofit organization committed to bridging the digital divide and bringing the benefits of expanding technology to everyone. It was founded in September 1998 and has since served more than 500 clients. The organization is located in a central urban area in an underserved community.

The company was established to equip students with the skills to maximize in-demand information technology (IT) career opportunities. They operate more than 15 classes and labs in state-of-the-art facilities at their administrative center and partner locations.

Each certificate program is designed to train students in the knowledge and abilities that today's employers need. Their instructors are all certified IT instructors with current, real-world IT experience. Their programs create real value for its students by combining high quality education with authentic hands-on training from experienced IT engineers. All the courses prepare students for professional certification tests and more advance courses. Once introduced and familiarized with technology, students have the opportunity, through Digit All Systems' courses, to gain the most in-demand technology knowledge and professional certifications

Web site: www.digitallsystems.org

Phone: (443) 729-2469

36. EAST END NEIGHBORHOOD HOUSE

East End Individual Learning Center provides high expectations and respect for children and their talents through cultural awareness, independence, choice, and problem solving. The program was established in 1973 to meet the needs of the community for quality child care and the provision of educational programs for all children. Also, the child care offers foreign languages, cultural awareness, and academic enrichment for toddlers (18–36 months) and preschoolers. The daycare center has earned a reputation for excellence in care and teaching. East End Youth Services enhance children's learning during out-of-school hours. The program creates opportunities for children to engage in an extended day-learning program, as well as to practice social skills, make art, and discover their hidden talents and potential. A major component of this program is geared toward increasing socialization and cultural enrichment.

Web site: www.eenh.org

Phone: (216) 791-9378

37. EDUSERC (EDUCATORS SERVING THE COMMUNITY)

The Eduserc mission is to build an infrastructure of resources to strategically and creatively address needs in the community that involve education.

Eduserc allows people to realize their dreams by engaging in a customized process of quality career, professional, and workforce development opportunities that guarantees a destination in a chosen field.

It does this by replicating the essence of each industry, what sustains them and makes them exciting (e.g. culinary, finance, or even engineering) and customizing individuals' personal experiences and access to role models in these industries such that it educates and causes them to discover their dream and purpose in life.

Web site: www.eduserc.org

Phone: (301) 498-2899

38.   EVERYBODY WINS!

EVERYBODY WINS! is a national public-private partnership that provides structured one-on-one mentoring to low-income youth. Taking root in 16 states and Washington, DC, EVERYBODY WINS! has evolved from informal read-aloud sessions to four distinct literacy and mentoring programs: Power Lunch, Readers Are Leaders, Story Time, and EW! Book Clubs. EVERYBODY WINS! affiliates are helping bridge the literacy gap for more than 9,200 public school students across the country. Their goal is to reach 100,000. With EVERYBODY WINS! the equation is simple: one mentor, one child, one book at a time.

Web site: www.everybodywins.org

Phone: (781) 489-5910

39.   FREEDOM FOR YOUTH, INC.

Freedom for Youth, Inc. provides three specialized mentoring programs aimed at helping develop positive and productive potential for at-risk youth: The Omega Little Brothers Program Mentoring Program targets at-risk males ages 8–18 whose fathers are absent from the home and/or physiologically or psychologically disabled. This program operates under a special three-to-one matching ratio, which allows one adult to work with three males in a small-group setting. This program provides intensive structure and ensures weekly group sessions that include psychosocial educational development, academic enrichment with tutorial support, recreation, art appreciation, and social skills development. Freedom for Youth, Inc. provides a comprehensive battery of services aimed at improving social skills for at-risk males and females who participate in the Freedom for Youth mentoring component. The primary focus is to help youth develop self-dignity and respect for themselves and others under the guidance of a faith-based program. Freedom for Youth continues to provide parent enrichment activities especially for the parents of youths who are currently in the various mentoring components. The focus is on empowering families to be all they can be by taking a holistic approach to service delivery. Thus, the program focuses not only on parenting, but also on helping parents with health and wellness issues, job development, and social skills development.

Web site: www.freedomforyouth.net

Phone: (870) 338-8781

40. **GAINING EARLY AWARENESS AND READINESS FOR UNDERGRADUATE PROGRAMS (GEAR UP)**

This discretionary U.S. Department of Education grant program is designed to increase the number of low-income students who are prepared to enter and succeed in postsecondary education. GEAR UP provides six-year grants to states and partnerships to deliver services to high-poverty middle and high schools. GEAR UP grantees serve an entire cohort of students beginning no later than the seventh grade and follows them through high school. GEAR UP funds are also used to provide college scholarships to low-income students.

Web site: www2.ed.gov/programs/gearup/
index.html

Phone: (800) USA-LEARN [(800) 872-5327]

41. **HARLEM RBI**

Harlem RBI's mission is to provide inner-city youth with opportunities to Play, Learn, and Grow. It uses the power of teams to coach, teach, and inspire youth to recognize their potential and realize their dreams. As a model learning community, it demonstrates how youth can become healthy, educated, and active global citizens who can achieve excellence and change the world. At Harlem RBI, social work does not just happen in the counseling office. It happens on the ball field, in the classroom, and over pizza. As a source of support that cares about youth performance in schools, neighborhoods, and in their families, Harlem RBI's Teen Life Center offers social services that address the complex needs of young people, including targeted workshops, short-term counseling or referrals, and crisis intervention. The Center's social workers also provide staff and volunteer training to ensure that the needs of our youth are met.

Web site: www.harlemrbi.org

Phone: (212) 722-1608

42.   HOSTS Corp (Help One Student to Succeed)

The HOSTS Structured Mentoring Program in Language Arts is a nationally recognized program that pairs a student who needs help in reading or math with a community member who wants to make a difference in a student's life. With help from volunteer mentors, students receive the extra attention and encouragement they need to become better students. HOSTS Corp is an active program under the Texas Youth Commission, the state's juvenile corrections agency. TYC strives to be a model juvenile corrections organization, providing protection for the public, a safe environment for youth and staff, and residential and parole services to the most serious juvenile delinquents in Texas. TYC forms partnerships with other state and local agencies, community groups, and individuals to develop and improve processes that reduce and prevent juvenile crime.

Web site: www.tyc.state.tx.us

Phone: (512) 424-6130

43. HOWARD UNIVERSITY SCHOOL OF EDUCATION

The mission of Howard University's School of Education is to: prepare teachers, administrators, researchers, program evaluators, and human development professionals for leadership in urban and diverse educational settings; significantly influence the national education agenda for African American children; conduct and disseminate research that supports the belief that all students can learn; and provide a research-based blueprint for developing professionals who are capable of creating environments that foster the abilities and talents of all students.

Web site: www.howard.edu/schooleducation/index.html

Phone: (202) 806-7340

44.   "I Have a Dream" Foundation

The "I Have A Dream" Foundation works to ensure that all children have the opportunity to pursue higher education. They empower children in low-income communities to achieve higher education by providing them with guaranteed tuition support and equipping them with the skills, knowledge, and habits they need to gain entry to higher education and succeed in college and beyond. By helping "Dreamers" gain access to college, they are putting them on a different academic and life trajectory, while having a broader impact on the students' families and the generations that follow. Dreamers have gone on to become teachers, social workers, secretaries, scholar-athletes, lawyers, and more. In many sites, they have doubled or tripled the local high school graduation and college enrollment rates. Their approach is unique in that they sponsor cohorts of students in under-resourced public schools or housing developments, and work with these Dreamers from early elementary school all the way through high school. Upon high school graduation, each Dreamer receives guaranteed tuition assistance for higher education.

Web site: www.ihaveadreamfoundation.org
Phone: (212) 293-5480

45.   IMPACT

IMPACT is the evaluation system for the nearly 6,500 school-based personnel in the District of Columbia Public Schools. First introduced in 2009, the system is based on the belief that the adults serving in the schools have the ability to make a dramatic, positive impact on students' lives. IMPACT is designed to help staff become more effective. This system holds educators accountable for the growth their students make on state assessments, or on other assessments, by: 1. Clarifying Expectations; 2. Providing Feedback and Support; and 3. Retaining Great People. IMPACT also provides data that helps instructional coaches, mentors, and other support personnel be more effective in their work.

Web site: www.dc.gov/DCPS/
In+the+Classroom/
Ensuring+Teacher+Success

Phone: (202) 442-5885

46.   INSTITUTE FOR INTERACTIVE INSTRUCTION

The Institute for Interactive Instruction, Inc. (Institute) is a non-partisan, 501(c) (3), nonprofit organization dedicated to creating a fundamental change in the community of organizations, programs, professionals, and community members

179

that care for children, youth, and families. In fostering a youth development model among adults, the Institute advocates for all young people with the hope of moving them higher on the nation's agenda.

Web site: www.iiiinc.org/index.php

Phone: (301) 776-4294

47. INSTITUTE FOR THE STUDY OF THE AFRICAN-AMERICAN CHILD (ISAAC)

The Institute for the Study of the African-American Child (ISAAC), College of Education, Wayne State University, fosters African American education and child development through research, dissemination of information, training, community service to parents, and clinical services for children. ISAAC strives to expand awareness and understanding of critical issues related to the achievement of African American children by illuminating policy issues at the local, state, and national levels.

Web site: education.wayne.edu/isaac/isaacsite/

Phone: (248) 661-4339

48. INTERNATIONAL TELEMENTOR PROGRAM

The International Telementor Program (ITP) facilitates online mentoring relationships be-

tween professional adults and students worldwide, and is recognized as the leader in the field
of academic based mentoring. Since 1995 over
40,000 students throughout nine countries have
received support, encouragement, and professional guidance. ITP serves students in K–12 and
home school environments as well as college and
university settings. Telementoring combines the
proven practice of mentoring with the speed and
ease of electronic communication, enabling busy
professionals to make significant contributions to
the academic lives of students. Through mentoring by industry professionals, a corporation helps
students develop the skills and foundation to
pursue their interests successfully and operate at
their potential.

Web site: www.telementor.org

Phone: (970) 481-9795

49.   JACK AND JILL OF AMERICA, INC.

The objectives of Jack and Jill of America,
Incorporated, are to "create a medium of contact
for children that stimulates growth and development and provide children a constructive educational, cultural, civic, health, recreational and
social programs." Since 1938 these objectives
have been at the forefront of the development

of children, particularly in the African American community.

Jack and Jill of America is a membership organization of mothers with children ages 2–19, dedicated to nurturing future leaders by supporting children through leadership development, volunteer service, philanthropic giving, and civic duty. Jack and Jill of America, Inc., has a special community service project designed to call attention to the current global state of the human habitat and push toward adequate housing for all. The Foundation supports programs that not only create opportunities and challenges for children to learn and practice leadership skills, but also build leadership character in youth. The ultimate goal is to empower young people to make the right life choices.

Web site: www.jackandjillinc.org

Phone: (202) 232-5290

50. JOBS FOR AMERICA'S GRADUATES (JAG)

Jobs for America's Graduates, Inc. (JAG), a national nonprofit corporation, serves young people faced with barriers to success. The more barriers a young person might have, the more he or she is considered "at risk" of not graduating from high school or having a successful transition from school to an entry-level job that leads to a career.

JAG's programs keep at-risk youth in middle school and high school through graduation; assist graduates in securing an entry-level job leading to career advancement opportunities; encourage and help graduates pursue a postsecondary education; and provide program participants with competency-based classroom experiences, recognition, and leadership opportunities.

Web site: www.jag.org

Phone: (617) 728-4446

51. JOBS FOR THE FUTURE (JFF) : EDUCATION FOR ECONOMIC OPPORTUNITY

JFF identifies, develops, and promotes education and workforce strategies that expand employment opportunity for youth and adults who are struggling to advance in America today. In more than 200 communities across 43 states, JFF improves the pathways leading from high school to college to family-sustaining careers. By 2020, JFF, working with its partners, is committed to doubling the number of low-income youth and adults who attain postsecondary credentials.

Web site: www.jff.org

Phone: (617) 728-4446

52. JUNIOR ACHIEVEMENT USA (JA)

Junior Achievement is the world's largest organization dedicated to educating students about workforce readiness, entrepreneurship, and financial literacy through experiential, hands-on programs. JA programs help prepare young people for the real world by showing them how to generate wealth and effectively manage it, how to create jobs that make their communities more robust, and how to apply entrepreneurial thinking to the workplace. Students put these lessons into action and learn the value of contributing to their communities. JA's unique approach allows volunteers from the community to deliver their curriculum while sharing their experiences with students. Embodying the heart of JA, their 382,637 classroom volunteers transform the key concepts of their lessons into a message that inspires and empowers students to believe in themselves, showing them they can make a difference in the world.

Web site: www.ja.org

Phone: (719) 540-8000

53. JUST US BOOKS

Just Us Books, Inc. is an independent publishing company specializing in books and learning materials for children and young people. It focuses on Black history, heritage and experiences. Founded by Wade Hudson and Cheryl Willis Hudson in 1988, this innovative company is now considered one of the leading publishers of Black interest titles for young people.

Just Us Books has had a major impact on the publishing industry from its inception. When the company released its first title, *AFRO-BETS® ABC Book*, there were very few Black interest books being published and widely distributed. From the start the company was dedicated to ensuring that these books would be available throughout the year—not just during Black History Month; to providing a creative venue for talented Black writers, illustrators, designers, and other professionals; and most importantly to inspiring, encouraging and educating young people through reading by offering books with characters, stories, and themes that reflected their lives as young Black people. The pioneering efforts of the Hudsons have helped to demonstrate that there is a viable market for Black interest books for children and young adults.

Web site: http://justusbooks.com/

54.   KAPOW: KIDS AND THE POWER OF WORK

KAPOW: Kids and the Power of Work is a program of the National Child Labor Committee, a national network of business and elementary school partnerships that introduces students to career awareness through professionally developed lessons taught by business volunteers in the classroom. In addition, students make one visit to the workplace to participate in hands-on activities. KAPOW® lays a foundation for young students, introducing them to work-related concepts and experiences that can be continually reinforced throughout the formative years.

KAPOW has developed a system of affiliates, which include local Chambers of Commerce, School-to-Work offices, or other nonprofits willing to act as the "governing entity" of the program. Full-fledged KAPOW affiliation is a three-year process during which a national KAPOW representative works with the affiliate and identified local coordinators to prepare them for increasing "ownership" of the community's KAPOW partnerships.

Web site: www.kapow.org

Phone: (212) 840-1801

55. KNOWLEDGE IS POWER PROGRAM (KIPP)

KIPP, the Knowledge Is Power Program, is a national network of free, open-enrollment, college-preparatory public schools with a track record of preparing students in underserved communities for success in college and in life. There are currently 109 KIPP schools in 20 states and the District of Columbia serving more than 32,000 students. KIPP builds a partnership among parents, students, and teachers that puts learning first. By providing outstanding educators, more time in school learning, and a strong culture of achievement, KIPP is helping all students climb the mountain to and through college. There are 61 KIPP middle schools (grades 5–8), 30 elementary schools (grades Pre-K–4), and 18 high schools (grades 9–12). Students are accepted regardless of prior academic record, conduct, or socioeconomic background.

Web site: www.kipp.org

Phone: (866) 345-KIPP [(866) 345-5477]

56.   LEARNING FOR LIFE

Learning for Life programs are designed for all age groups from pre-kindergarten through age 20. Youth participation is open to any youth in the prescribed age group for that particular program. LFL's mission is to develop and deliver engaging, research-based academic-, character-, leadership-, and career-focused programs aligned to state and national standards that guide and enable all students to achieve their full potential.

Learning for Life's team of educators have developed a supplemental PreK–12 educational program that uniquely integrates its well-recognized character-development program with the core academic content areas of reading, math, science, and social studies. The Learning for Life integrated academic and character development program has been shown to improve academic proficiency, attendance, graduation rates, and the overall campus climate.

Web site: www.learningforlife.org

Phone: (855) 806-9992

57. LINKS, INC.

The Links, Incorporated, is an international, not-for-profit corporation, established in 1946. The membership consists of 12,000 professional women of color in 274 chapters located in 42 states, the District of Columbia, and the Commonwealth of the Bahamas. It is one of the nation's oldest and largest volunteer service organizations of extraordinary women who are committed to enriching, sustaining, and ensuring the culture and economic survival of African Americans and other persons of African ancestry.

Today, The Links continues to implement programs that are responsive to the academic, cultural, health, social awareness, career development, and mentoring needs of youth. The Links has entered into a national partnership with National Cares Mentoring Movement (NCMM). Through this partnership, local chapters support NCMM's commitment to closing the gap between the number of African American adult mentors and the millions of willing African American children on the waiting lists of mentoring organizations throughout the nation.

Web site: www.linksinc.org

Phone: (202) 842-8686

58. MAD DADS, INC.

MAD DADS is an acronym for Men Against Destruction Defending Against Drugs and Social-Disorder. MAD DADS, INC. was founded in May of 1989 by a group of concerned Omaha, Nebraska, parents who were fed up with gang violence and the unmolested flow of illegal drugs in their community.

MAD DADS are positive role models and concerned loving parents who are a visible presence in neighborhoods against the negative forces destroying children, families, and cities. MAD DADS realizes that we could hold no one responsible but ourselves. So they united as a handful of community fathers whose mission is to bring about positive change; seek out, encourage, motivate, and guide committed men in the struggle to save children, communities, and ourselves from the social ills that presently plague neighborhoods. MAD DADS employs strategies to engage parents in the intervention and prevention of community problems, and is designed to attract, challenge, and prepare them to be vocal, visible, and vigilant in restoring safe communities and healthy families.

Web site: www.maddads.com

59. MENTOR/National Mentoring Partnership

MENTOR: The National Mentoring Partnership (MENTOR) has been the lead champion for youth mentoring in the United States. MENTOR helps children by providing a public voice; developing and delivering resources to mentoring programs nationwide; and promoting quality for mentoring through standards, cutting-edge research, and state-of-the-art tools.

MENTOR works closely with State Mentoring Partnerships and more than 5,000 mentoring programs and volunteer centers throughout the country, serving more than 3 million children in all 50 states. There are currently 18 million children in the United States who want and need a mentor, but only 3 million have one. MENTOR's mission is to close that gap so that every one of those 15 million children has a caring adult in their life.

Web site: www.mentoring.org

Phone: (202) 347-2080

60. MENTORING USA

Mentoring USA's mission is to create sustained and supportive mentor relationships for children in need ages 7–21. The program matches youth across the country with inspirational adult mentors who can guide them in developing better self-esteem, creating healthy relationships, and making positive life choices. Many youth enter the program experiencing varying levels of educational difficulties or social challenges. Mentoring USA has special programs to target youth-in-care and adopted youth.

Web site: www.mentoringusa.org

Phone: (212) 400-8294

61.   MODELS FOR CHANGE

Models for Change collaborates with selected states to advance juvenile justice reforms that effectively hold young people accountable for their actions, provide for their rehabilitation, protect them from harm, increase their life chances, and manage the risk they pose to themselves and to public safety.

Web site: www.modelsforchange.net/index.
html

Phone: (312) 726-8000

62.   NATIONAL 4-H COUNCIL

4-H is the nation's largest youth development organization. More than 6 million 4-H youth in urban neighborhoods, suburban schoolyards, and rural farming communities stand out among their peers by building revolutionary opportunities and implementing community-wide change at an early age. As the youth development program of the nation's 109 land-grant universities and the Cooperative Extension System, 4-H fosters an innovative "learn by doing" approach with proven results. Research confirms that youth engaged with 4-H are: nearly two times more likely to get better grades in school, nearly two times more likely to plan to go to college, 41 percent less likely to engage in risky behaviors, and 25 percent more likely to positively contribute to their families and communities.

Web site: www.fourhcouncil.edu

63. NATIONAL AFRICAN AMERICAN DRUG POLICY COALITION (NAADPC)

The National African American Drug Policy Coalition is a coalition of pre-eminent African American professional organizations united to promote drug policies and laws that embrace the public health nature of drug abuse, and provide a more effective and humane approach to address the chronic societal problem of drug abuse. It has a special commitment to implementation of drug abuse policies and practices that advance the protection of the nation's children, reduce crime, and improve public safety and order.

Web site: www.naadpc.org

Phone: (202) 806-8600

64. NATIONAL ALLIANCE FOR PUBLIC CHARTER SCHOOLS

The National Alliance for Public Charter Schools is the leading organization committed to advancing quality, growth, and sustainability for the charter school movement. Their approach to advocacy and national reach allows them to impact charter schools at both the federal and state levels. This organization speaks and advocates for the hundreds of thousands of students who are hoping for the chance to attend a charter school. They provide assistance to state charter school associations and resource centers, develop and advocate for improved public policies, and serve as the united voice for this large and diverse movement.

Web site: www.publiccharters.org

Phone: (202) 289-2700

65. NATIONAL ASSOCIATION FOR THE EDUCATION OF AFRICAN AMERICAN CHILDREN WITH LEARNING DISABILITIES

The AACLD was founded by a mother and her two sons for the purpose of increasing awareness in minority communities about learning differences and promoting parent advocacy. The AACLD serves thousands of African American families throughout the United States. In addition, it has continued to serve the broader public by responding to an extraordinary number of requests for information nationwide from a very diverse audience including teachers, public and private K–12 schools, colleges and universities, social service agencies, psychologists, hospitals, churches, lawyers, parent groups, and other organizations.

Web site: http://aacld.org/

Phone: (614) 237-6021

66. **NATIONAL ASSOCIATION OF PARTNERS IN EDUCATION**

The National Association of Partners in Education has been an objective voice in developing school volunteer, intergenerational, community service, and business partnership programs throughout the United States. It is the only national membership organization devoted solely to providing leadership in the field of education partnership development. To improve opportunities for comprehensive youth development, Partners in Education works to increase the number, quality, and scope of effective partnerships; increase the resources to support effective partnerships; increase awareness about the importance of partnerships for promoting youth success; and promote the importance of effective partnerships to policy makers. Efforts are focused through three core competencies: Training and Technical Assistance, Research and Materials Development, and Unique National Member Network. Grassroots Leadership: Partners in Education has direct links to local school districts and community leaders throughout the country. Through thousands of grassroots member programs, Partners in Education connects children and classroom teachers with corporate, education, volunteer, government, and civic leaders. These community partners play significant roles in changing the content and delivery of education services to children and their families.

Web site: www.napehq.org/1.html

67. NATIONAL ASSOCIATION OF POLICE ATHLETIC LEAGUES

PAL is a youth-crime prevention program that utilizes educational, athletic, and recreational activities to create trust and understanding between police officers and youth. It is based on the conviction that young people—if they are reached early enough—can develop strong positive attitudes toward police officers in their journey through life toward the goal of maturity and good citizenship. The PAL program brings youth under the supervision and positive influence of a law enforcement agency; it expands public awareness about the role of police officers and the reinforcement of the responsible values and attitudes instilled in young people by their parents. National PAL provides chapter members opportunities to bring their young athletes together to compete in a championship environment in several sports.

Web site: www.nationalpal.org

Phone: (561) 745-5535

68.   NATIONAL BLACK PARENTS ASSOCIATION

The NBPA works to eliminate the achievement gap and bring equality and reform to public education. Among its many advocacy objectives, NBPA strives to mobilize Black parents into a unified force that can effectively lobby local education boards, state education agencies, state legislators, and Congress for programs, policies, and changes that are advantageous for Black students, empower Black parents to be more effectively involved in the education of their children and to develop effective strategies to elect more Black parents to local school boards, P.T.A.s, booster clubs, etc.

Web site: http://nbpa.info/

69.   NATIONAL COLLABORATION FOR YOUTH

National Collaboration for Youth (NCY) is the longest-standing coalition of national organizations committed to advocating with and on behalf of youth and, in particular, in research-driven "positive youth development." In NCY, youth are defined by their assets and potential, not by their challenges. "The Collab" is devoted to positive youth development in the areas of policy, practice, and research.

Web site: www.collab4youth.org

Phone: (202) 347-2080

70. **NATIONAL COUNCIL ON EDUCATING BLACK CHILDREN (NCEBC)**

The National Council on Educating Black Children (NCEBC) is a premier nonprofit and civil rights organization with a distinguished focus on improving educational opportunities and outcomes for African American children. By galvanizing "coalitions of the willing," NCEBC is aggressively implementing solutions that elevate communities by empowering stakeholders who are ready to "take responsibility" for their villages.

The NCEBC Augustus F. Hawkins Literacy Centers are designed to enhance the instruction provided by public and charter schools to those students who are classified as at high risk for academic failure. Because research indicates there is a high correlation between illiteracy and incarceration, these centers are being located in zip codes characterized by high crime, violence, low socio-economics, and households headed by single females.

NCEBC's Parent University Curriculum is the model for parent advocacy and student voices. The Parent University Curriculum is a series of workshops and professional development activities that will increase the knowledge and skills needed to "build the public will" on behalf of African American children.

Web site: ncebc.org

Phone: (317) 283-9081

71. NATIONAL DROPOUT PREVENTION CENTER/ NETWORK

The National Dropout Prevention Center/ Network (NDPC/N) serves as a clearinghouse on issues related to dropout prevention and offers strategies designed to increase the graduation rate in America's schools. NDPC/N has become a well-established national resource for sharing solutions for student success. Since 1987, the National Dropout Prevention Center/Network has worked to improve opportunities for all young people to fully develop the academic, social, work, and healthy life skills needed to graduate from high school and lead productive lives.

Web site: www.dropoutprevention.org

Phone: (864) 656-2599

72. NATIONAL EDUCATION ASSOCIATION (SAFE SCHOOL STRATEGIES)

NEA believes every student in America, regardless of family income or place of residence, deserves a quality education. In pursuing its mission, NEA has determined that they will focus the energy and resources of their 3.2 million members on improving the quality of teaching; increasing student achievement; and making schools safer, better places to learn.

Web site: www.nea.org

Phone: (202) 833-4000

73. NATIONAL FATHERHOOD INITIATIVE

National Fatherhood Initiative strives to improve the well-being of children by increasing the proportion of children growing up with involved, responsible, and committed fathers. They strive to ensure a brighter future for America's youth. By equipping and educating fathers, they're working on an issue that is at the core of our nation's well-being.

Web site: www.fatherhood.org

Phone: (301) 948-0599

74. NATIONAL PARENT TEACHER ASSOCIATION

As the largest volunteer child advocacy association in the nation, the Parent Teacher Association (PTA) reminds our country of its obligations to children and provides parents and families with a powerful voice to speak on behalf of every child while providing the best tools for parents to help their children be successful students. Working in cooperation with many national education, health, safety, and child advocacy groups and federal agencies, the national PTA organization collaborates on projects that benefit children and bring valuable resources to its members.

Web site: www.pta.org

Phone: (703) 518-1200, Toll Free: (800) 307-4PTA (4782)

75. National Resource Center on Children and Families of the Incarcerated

The mission of the National Resource Center on Children and Families of the Incarcerated (NRCCFI) at Family and Corrections Network (FCN) is to raise awareness about the needs and concerns of the children of the incarcerated and their families by providing information informed by a combination of academic research and the real-life experiences of the families and practitioners in the field in order to promote the creation of effective and relevant policies and practices.

Web site: http://fcnetwork.org/

Phone: (215) 576-1110

76. National Urban Coalition for Unity and Peace

The mission of the National Urban Coalition for Unity and Peace, Inc. is to expose children from local communities to innovative educational programs, artistic projects, recreational excursions, and community ventures that empower them to compete globally and become productive members of society.

Their comprehensive programs include youth initiatives and training; addressing at-risk children and families; providing community services to senior citizens; increasing public safety and awareness; working diligently to improve the skills and education of targeted inner-city populations; and creating a climate that provides a sense of togetherness among community residents. NUC has a viable and results-oriented after-school program designed to reinforce a young person's sense of peace and safety. Activities are designed to allow children time to relax, develop socialization skills, and realize their impact in team building. Participants receive homework assistance and are provided with tips for successful test taking.

Web site: www.nucup.org

Phone: (404) 669-0204

77.   NATIONAL URBAN LEAGUE (NUL)

The National Urban League is a historic civil rights organization dedicated to economic empowerment in order to elevate the standard of living in historically underserved urban communities. Headquartered in New York City, the National Urban League spearheads the efforts of its local affiliates through the development of programs, public policy research, and advocacy. Today, there are more than 100 local affiliates in 36 states and the District of Columbia, providing direct services that impact and improve the lives of more than 2 million people nationwide.

Web site: www.nul.org

Phone: (212) 558-5300

78. New Leaders for New Schools

New Leaders for New Schools was founded in 2000 by a team of social entrepreneurs. It attracts, prepares, and supports outstanding individuals to become the next generation of school leaders in response to the immense need for exceptional principals in our nation's urban public schools. New Leaders for New Schools is a national movement of leaders with an unwavering commitment to ensuring that every student achieves academic excellence.

Web site: www.nlns.org

Phone: (646) 792-1070

79. Office of Juvenile Justice and Delinquency Prevention

Juveniles in crisis—from serious, violent, and chronic offenders to victims of abuse and neglect—pose a challenge to the nation. Charged by Congress to meet this challenge, OJJDP collaborates with professionals from diverse disciplines to improve juvenile justice policies and practices.

OJJDP, a component of the Office of Justice Programs, U.S. Department of Justice, accomplishes its mission by supporting states, local communities, and tribal jurisdictions in their efforts to develop and implement effective programs for juveniles. The Office strives to strengthen the juvenile justice system's efforts to protect public safety, hold offenders accountable, and provide services that address the needs of youth and their families. OJJDP also sponsors research, program, and training initiatives; develops priorities and goals and sets policies to guide federal juvenile justice issues; disseminates information about juvenile justice issues; and awards funds to states to support local programming.

Web site: www.ojjdp.govindex.html

Phone: (202) 307-5911

80. OMEGA BOYS CLUB/STREET SOLDIERS

The Omega Boys Club/Street Soldiers mission is to keep young people alive and unharmed by violence and free from incarceration. It provides youth with opportunity and support to build positive lives for themselves and to move into contributing roles in society.

The Omega Training Institute program trains individuals and professionals in violence prevention/conflict reduction skills, based on the Omega Boys Club/Street Soldiers model. The Institute has three programs. The School Adoption Program works with Bay Area schools, helping them transform their classrooms so they can achieve a violence-free learning environment and academic success. Omega Training Institutes inform, teach and train individuals who work with youth in the Alive & Free violence prevention prescription developed by the Omega Boys Club. The Street Soldiers National Consortium is a group of professionals and organizations trained in the Omega violence prevention methodology and dedicated to preventing violence by using and promoting the model.

Web site: www.street-soldiers.org

Phone: (415) 826-8664

81. **OPEN SOCIETY FOUNDATIONS, CAMPAIGN FOR BLACK MALE ACHIEVEMENT**

The Campaign for Black Male Achievement is a multi-issue, cross-fund strategy to address Black men and boys' exclusion from economic, social, educational, and political life in the United States. The campaign responds to a growing body of research that reveals the intensification of Black males' negative life outcomes.

Building on its long commitment to reverse systemic injustices in the United States, the Open Society Foundation recently announced that it is joining a new three-year $30 million initiative to address broad disparities and transform the lives of Black and Latino boys and men in New York City. The Open Society Foundations supports a diverse set of programs—including those focusing on the "school-to-prison" pipeline.

Web site: www.soros.org/initiatives/usprograms /focus/cbma

Phone: (212) 548-0600

82. PATRIOT'S TECHNOLOGY TRAINING CENTER (PTTC)

"Empowering Students Through Technology" has been their mission for twelve years (5th to 12th grades) by increasing the number of students entering science, mathematics, engineering, and computer technology leading to college education and career paths in those interrelated fields. Over the years they have partnered with some of the major technology, government and foundations to support their mission.

Their program has stemmed from having a Youth Summit on Technology, Summer Camp, and After School Programs. They also engage in Lego, Robotics, Tri-Math-A-Lon and Science Bowl competitions.

Web site: www.patriots-ttc.org

Phone: (301) 925-9350

83.   Peace First

Peace First is dedicated to building effective school climates by focusing on two major efforts within a school: teaching children the skills of conflict resolution and civic engagement, and providing educators with the critical skills and knowledge to integrate social-emotional learning into the school's curriculum and culture. Combined, these efforts strengthen schools' social and academic environments, creating stronger schools and more successful students.

Web site: www.peacefirst.org

Phone: National Office / Peace First Boston: (617) 261-3833
Peace First Los Angeles: (213) 443-3115
Peace First New York: (617) 261-3833

84.   Phi Delta Kappa International

Phi Delta Kappa International is the premier professional association for educators. For more than 100 years, it has focused its work on the tenets of service, research, and leadership. PDK is one of the largest education associations in the world and has thousands of members dedicated to improving education—including teachers, principals, superintendents, and higher education faculty and administrators. PDK's mission is to support education, particularly public education, as the cornerstone of democracy. Its vision is to be the experts in cultivating great educators for tomorrow while continuing to ensure high quality education for today.

Web site: http://www.pdkintl.org/index.htm

Phone: (800) 766-1156

85. PROMISING PRACTICES NETWORK

The Promising Practices Network (PPN) is a group of individuals and organizations who are dedicated to providing quality evidence-based information about what works to improve the lives of children, families, and communities.

A research-rich portal operated by a core team from the RAND Corporation, PPN provides current information on programs that work, and also links to additional research information in all areas related to child well-being, including their physical and mental health, academic success, and economic security.

RAND brings to PPN extensive experience in the child policy arena, with more than 150 researchers and consultants working in areas such as child health, juvenile justice, education, child care, labor, and demographics. RAND's analysis has shaped public policy on a range of problems facing young people and helps decision-makers understand what approaches and programs have been shown in the scientific literature to improve outcomes in areas such as child health and education.

Web site: www.promisingpractices.net

Phone: (310) 393-0411, ext 7172

86.   PRO-VISION, INC.

Pro-Vision addresses the needs of young men ages 11–18 that are underserved by society and are at risk of dropping out of school. Pro-Vision takes students who are two grade levels behind and alters their self-perception by creating a community that emphasizes social skills, self-awareness, and a solid work ethic. Students have the opportunity to be guided, challenged, and supported by adults who are not just classroom teachers, but who are conveyers of the organization's core principles of affirming students' innate worth and helping them to recognize their abilities.

Web site: www.provision-inc.org

Phone: (713) 748-0030

87.   PUBLIC ALLIES

Public Allies advances new leadership to strengthen communities, nonprofits, and civic participation. It has developed a new generation of diverse leaders and promoted innovative leadership practices that meet the demands of our changing times. Public Allies' citizen-centered, values-based approach to leadership emphasizing personal and social responsibility has created pathways for young people to engage in their communities, and has helped communities and organizations tap the energy, passion, and perspectives of a new generation. Public Allies' signature AmeriCorps Ally Program identifies diverse young adults and prepares them for leadership through paid, full-time nonprofit apprenticeships and rigorous leadership training.

Web site: www.publicallies.org

Phone: (414) 273-0533

88.   QUALITY EDUCATION FOR MINORITIES (QEM)

The Quality Education for Minorities (QEM) Network is a nonprofit organization based in Washington, DC, dedicated to improving the education of African Americans, Alaska Natives, American Indians, Mexican Americans, and

Puerto Ricans. Quality education for minorities improves the quality of education for all. QEM recognizes the enormous potential of public policy to achieve quality education for children and youth who have been historically underserved by the educational system. QEM's aim is to create more effective policy as well as a vehicle for action that leads to quality education for minorities.

Web site: www.qem.org

Phone: (202) 659-1818

89.   Raising Him Alone

The Raising Him Alone Campaign is a national initiative designed to support single mothers raising boys in some of the toughest communities throughout this country. It draws on the experiences of single mothers across the U.S. to create inspiring focus groups, community forums, workshops, and support group initiatives. There has been a historical disregard for the voices of single mothers living in urban communities. Such neglect of mothers raising boys has created some alarming trends among African American boys. To reverse this trend, the campaign has advocated for single mothers' increased access to services (mental health, financial literacy, and strategies for parenting a male child) that will ensure positive outcomes for African American boys.

Web site: www.raisinghimalone.com/index.
htm

Phone: (877) 339-4300

90. RESIDENTIAL AFTER-SCHOOL PROGRAM (RASP)

RASP is a national organization devoted to the education of parents, teachers, and students about their potential on the growth of young men and women of minority background through after-school education throughout the academic calendar. From first grade to high school, through after-school and supplementary academic courses and conferences, RASP allows for greater comprehension and progression of academic-level material as well as work application and experience. RASP offers an array of services that help school districts increase parental involvement and address Title I Funding objectives. Services include design and promotion of parent conferences and lectures, and facilitation of professional training workshops and services.

Web site: www.raspinc.org

Phone: (732) 208-9808

91. SAVE THE CHILDREN (STC)

Save the Children is the leading independent organization creating lasting change in the lives of children in need in the United States and around the world. Recognized for its commitment to accountability, innovation, and collaboration, its work takes it into the heart of communities, where it helps children and families help themselves. STC works with other organizations, governments, nonprofits, and a variety of local partners while maintaining its own independence without political agenda or religious orientation. Save the Children's education programs reach children at risk—girls; ethnic minorities; and children affected by rural poverty, HIV/AIDS, conflict, and natural disasters—from early childhood through young adulthood. The STC focus is on communities in greatest need, designing programs that make it easy to participate, even for children who work or have missed years of schooling; preparing toddlers for school; and making the curriculum meaningful to children's lives and addressing the special needs of children with disabilities.

Save the Children is committed to raising literacy rates by supporting early childhood development programs and believes that children must also be well nourished and healthy in order to learn.

Web site: www.savethechildren.org

Phone: (800) 728-3843

92.   SCHOLASTIC, INC.

Scholastic, the global children's publishing, education, and media company, has a corporate mission supported through all of its divisions of helping children around the world to read and learn. Scholastic aims to help build a society free of prejudice and hate, and is dedicated to the highest quality of life in community and nation. It strives to present the clearest explanation of current affairs and contemporary thought, and to encourage literary appreciation and expression consistent with the understanding and interests of young people at all levels of learning.

Web site: www.scholastic.com

Phone: (573) 636-5271

93.   STAND UP CAMPAIGN

STAND UP is an education nonprofit dedicated to ensuring every child has the opportunity to attend an excellent public school. In 2009, STAND UP became a featured initiative of new Sacramento Mayor Kevin Johnson. STAND UP believes in order to ensure that young people are prepared to be productive citizens in the 21st century and competitive in the global marketplace, the problems of low expectations, low high school graduation rates, truancy, lack of compelling and engaging school options, and the persistent achievement gap must be addressed. Traditionally, the city has been most involved in programs outside of school hours such as work-study opportunities and after-school programs.

Web site: www.standup.org

Email: Info@StandUp.org

94.   STATES FOR CHANGE

States for Change is an initiative of Models for Change that includes the selection of four strategic states identified for their leadership and commitment to change, geographic diversity, differing needs and opportunities, and likelihood to influence reforms in other locations. An additional 12 states (including Maryland, Wisconsin, Kansas, North Carolina, California, Florida, Massachusetts, and New Jersey) are involved and participate in the Models for Change action networks. Models for Change is now a 16-state national initiative that advances juvenile justice system reforms that effectively hold young people accountable for their actions, provide for their rehabilitation, protect them from harm, increase their life chances, and manage the risk they pose.

Web site: www.modelsforchange.net/about/ States-for-change.html

95.   SUMMER ADVANTAGE USA

Summer Advantage USA is a nonprofit organization that runs high quality summer learning programs for children in grades K–8. The program focuses on academics and enrichment. Summer Advantage aims to provide children access to a well-rounded summer program that helps them succeed in school, stimulates their dreams for the future, and helps them develop as leaders in their communities.

Web site: www.summeradvantage.org

Phone: (866) 924-7226

96.   SUPPORTING ADOLESCENTS WITH GUIDANCE AND EMPLOYMENT (SAGE)

Supporting Adolescents with Guidance and Employment (SAGE) is a violence-prevention program developed specifically for African American adolescents. The program consists of three main components: a Rites of Passages (ROP) program, a summer jobs training and placement (JTP) program, and an entrepreneurial experience that uses the Junior Achievement (JA) model.

The ROP program promotes a strong sense of African American cultural pride, self-esteem, positive attitudes, and the avoidance of a range of risky behaviors. Instructors cover topics such as conflict resolution, African American history, male sexuality, and manhood training.

97. TEACH FOR AMERICA

Teach for America's mission is to eliminate inequity by developing exceptional leaders to provide exceptional education. Recruiting is done from college graduates of all backgrounds to teach for two years in urban and rural public schools. TFA provides intensive training, support, and career development that helps these teachers increase their impact and deepen their understanding of what it takes to close the achievement gap.

Web site: www.teachforamerica.org

Phone: (414) 273-1203

98. THE ACT 4 JUVENILE JUSTICE CAMPAIGN

Established in 1974, the Juvenile Justice and Delinquency Prevention Act (JJDPA) is a partnership between the federal government and the states to protect children and youth in the juvenile and criminal justice system, to effectively address high-risk and delinquent behavior, and improve community safety. Act 4 Juvenile Justice strives to: keep children and youth out of the juvenile and criminal justice systems whenever possible by addressing their needs, and those of their families, early and effectively; and to do everything possible to ensure equity, competence, and age-appropriate legal representation before the courts and throughout all system practices and policies.

Web site: www.act4jj.org

99. THE AFTER-SCHOOL INSTITUTE (TASI)

The After-School Institute helps after-school programs achieve the highest standards of performance. It is committed to strengthening the support system among after-school providers, families, teachers, and community organizations. TASI offers providers the training they need to meet quality standards established by the Baltimore After-School Strategy. Quality after-school programs should provide children with a safe, healthy atmosphere where they can explore new activities and ideas; build confidence, self-respect, awareness, and strong decision-making skills; and develop supportive, one-on-one relationships with both adults and peers.

Web site: www.afterschoolinstitute.org

Phone: (410) 580-0750

100. THE AFTERSCHOOL ALLIANCE

The nation's leading voice for afterschool, the Afterschool Alliance is the only organization dedicated to raising awareness of the importance of after-school programs and advocating for more after-school investments. The Afterschool Alliance works with more than 25,000 after-school program partners and its publications reach more than 65,000 interested individuals every month.

Web site: www.afterschoolalliance.org

Phone: (866) KIDS-TODAY

101. THE ALLIANCE FOR EXCELLENT EDUCATION

The Alliance for Excellent Education is a Washington, DC–based national policy and advocacy organization that works to improve national and federal policy so that all students can achieve at high academic levels and graduate from high school ready for success in college, work, and citizenship in the 21st century. The Alliance focuses on America's 6 million most at-risk secondary school students—those in the lowest achievement quartile—who are most likely to leave school without a diploma or to graduate unprepared for a productive future. The Alliance publishes many briefs, reports, and fact sheets; and hosts numerous events and makes presentations—in DC, on Capitol Hill, and around the country—to encourage public support and action. It also helps policy makers and the public understand the economic costs of an educational system that serves so many students poorly.

Web site: www.all4ed.org/about_the_crisis

Phone: (202) 828-0828

102. THE BLACK COMMUNITY CRUSADE FOR CHILDREN (BCCC)

The Children's Defense Fund's Black Community Crusade for Children (BCCC) was organized to confront a deepening crisis faced by Black children and is calling on America to take action. A toxic cocktail of poverty, illiteracy, racial disparity, violence, and massive incarceration is sentencing millions of children of color to dead-end, powerless, and hopeless lives, and threatens to undermine the past half-century of racial and social progress. Black children and youth continue to face multiple risks from birth and throughout life that increase the danger of their becoming part of the Cradle to Prison Pipeline® crisis that leads to dead-end lives. To highlight these harsh realities, CDF produced the "Portrait of Inequality 2011," a report showing the gross inequalities facing Black children compared to white children, across all critical indicators of well-being.

Web site: www.childrensdefense.org/programs-
campaigns/black-community-
crusade-for-children-II

Phone: (800) CDF-1200 [(800) 233-1200]

103. THE BLACK PARENT GROUP

The Black Parent Group provides culturally specific workshops to help parents and guardians address the underlying issues of the achievement gap, connect to local resources, and provide a safe place for parents to gain support. BPG offers mentoring to families, and provides staff trainings/ workshops on the best practices to employ with Black families.

Web site: http://theblackparentgroup.com/
default.aspx

104. THE BLACK PARENT INITIATIVE

The Black Parent Initiative inspires and mobilizes Black parents to ensure their children achieve educational excellence by helping families achieve financial, spiritual, and educational success. BPI is dedicated to inspiring, engaging, and mobilizing parents/caregivers to improve the educational outcomes of Black children. The Black Parent Initiative is a participatory, community-based organization and the guiding principle behind BPI is the strong need for more family specific support networks. BPI recognizes the untapped and strong powerbase of the Black church as a strong mediating institution. Its success as an organization is based largely upon member churches and partnering organizations.

Web site: www.thebpi.org

Phone: (503) 502-6790

105. THE BLACK PARENTS FORUM (BPF)

The Black Parents Forum (BPF) supports parents interested in pursuing academic excellence for their children. Black Parents Forum hosts Student Recruitment Fairs, Teacher of Color Recruitment Fairs, Summer Enrichment Fairs, and other information fairs throughout the school year in cities across the US.

Web site: http://www.blackparentsforum.info/

Phone: (404) 241-5003

106. THE BLACK STAR PROJECT

The Black Star Project is committed to improving the quality of life in Black and Latino communities of Chicago and nationwide by eliminating the racial academic achievement gap. Its mission is to provide educational services that help pre-school through college students, particularly low-income Black and Latino students who attend low-achieving schools in disadvantaged communities, succeed academically and become knowledgeable and productive citizens with the support of their parents, families, schools, and communities.

The Black Star Project operates with a belief in the strength of parental and community involvement. Better parents produce better communities, better schools, and better students! The most accurate predictor of a student's achievement is the extent to which a student's family is able to: create a home environment that encourages learning; express high and realistic academic achievement expectations for their children; and become involved in productive ways in their child's education at school, at home, and in the community. The Black Star Project works to address these areas and more.

Web site: blackstarproject.org/action/index. php

Phone: (773) 285-9600

107.   THE CAMPAIGN FOR GRADE-LEVEL READING

The Campaign for Grade-Level Reading is a national effort to combat alarmingly high rates of low-income children in the United States not reading proficiently by the end of 3rd grade—an early and leading indicator of high school completion and college attendance. The Campaign seeks to energize and mobilize a broad cross-section of community leaders to develop and implement community solutions to three of the major reasons that so many children miss the important milestone of grade-level reading by the end of third grade: (1) too many children are already too far behind when they start school; (2) too many children miss too many days of school; and (3) too many children lose too much ground during the summer months and return to school in the fall behind where they were in June.

Web site: www.gradelevelreading.net

Phone: (212) 548-0132

108. THE CAMPAIGN FOR YOUTH JUSTICE (CFYJ)

The CFYJ is dedicated to ending the practice of trying, sentencing, and incarcerating youth under 18 in the adult criminal justice system. The Campaign works in partnership with state-based campaigns in a number of geographic areas. CFYJ serves as a clearinghouse of information on youth prosecuted as adults and delivers tools and resources to those interested in learning and taking action on this issue. CFYJ is a member organization of the National Juvenile Justice and Delinquency Prevention Coalition (NJJDPC), a collaborative array of youth- and family-serving, social justice, law enforcement, corrections, and faith-based organizations, working to ensure healthy families, build strong communities, and improve public safety by promoting fair and effective policies, practices, and programs for youth involved or at risk of becoming involved in the juvenile and criminal justice systems.

Web site: www.campaignforyouthjustice.org

109. THE CENTER FOR CHILDREN'S LAW AND POLICY (CCLP)

The Center for Children's Law and Policy (CCLP) is a public interest law and policy organization focused on reform of juvenile justice and other systems that affect troubled and at-risk children, as well as protection of the rights of children in those systems. The Center's work covers a range of activities including research, writing, public education, media advocacy, training, technical assistance, administrative and legislative advocacy, and litigation.

The Network also offers jurisdictions the opportunity to exchange information about strategy implementation and data measurement.

Web site: www.cclp.org

Phone: (202) 637-0377

110. THE CENTER FOR SOCIAL ORGANIZATION OF SCHOOLS (CSOS)

The Center for Social Organization of Schools (CSOS), an educational research and development center, was established in 1966 at Johns Hopkins University. The purpose of the Center for Social Organization of Schools has remained consistent since its founding—to study how changes in the organization of schools can make them more effective for all students in promoting academic achievement, development of potential, and eventual career success. CSOS maintains a staff of full-time sociologists, psychologists, social psychologists, and educators who conduct programmatic research to improve the education system, develop curricula, and provide technical assistance to schools.

Web site: www.csos.jhu.edu

Phone: (410) 516-8800

111. THE COALITION FOR JUVENILE JUSTICE (CJJ)

The CJJ is a nationwide coalition of State Advisory Groups (SAGs) and allies dedicated to preventing children and youth from becoming involved in the courts and upholding the highest standards of care when youth are charged with wrongdoing and enter the justice system. The

Coalition's efforts include instituting juvenile justice system reforms to improve racial/ethnic fairness, as well as accessibility and overall quality of community- and court-based policies and practices.

Web site: http://juvjustice.njjn.org/about.html

112. THE COALITION OF SCHOOLS EDUCATING BOYS OF COLOR (COSEBOC)

COSEBOC is dedicated to reimagining and transforming the schooling experience for males of color. COSEBOC is a networked learning community of highly respected educators, researchers, policy makers, and caring adults. It supports school leaders with quality professional development so they can realize this vision of making success an attainable goal for every male student of color. COSEBOC is committed to high standards, exemplary instruction, and the building of coalitions within and outside the community that will allow boys of color to become fully equipped to achieve academically, socially, and emotionally.

Web site: www.coseboc.org/index.htm

Phone: (855) 267-3262

113. THE EAGLE ACADEMY FOUNDATION

The Eagle Academy Foundation develops and supports a network of all-male, grades 6–12, college-preparatory schools in challenged urban communities that educate and mentor young men into future leaders committed to excellence in character, scholastic achievement, and community service, and to promoting these principles nationally. The Eagle Academy Foundation empowers at-risk inner city young men to become academic achievers, engaged citizens, and responsible men by providing quality education resources and proven effective community-based initiatives to address the shortfalls in public education to effectively educate them.

Web site: http://eagleacademyfoundation.com/

Phone: (212) 477-8370

114. THE NATIONAL ASSOCIATION OF CHARTER SCHOOL AUTHORIZERS (NACSA)

NACSA is unique in the charter school movement. It is devoted exclusively to improving public education by improving the policies and practices of the organizations responsible for authorizing charter schools. Quality authorizing leads to quality charter schools, and NACSA is creating the environment of expectations, relationships, practices, policy, and resources for authorizers to excel.

NACSA works with local experts to create the conditions needed for quality schools to thrive. They push for high standards for authorizers and help to define successful authorizer practices.

NACSA believes that genuine reform through charter schools occurs through the balanced interplay of three principles: choice, autonomy, and accountability.

Web site: www.qualitycharters.org

Phone: (312) 376-2300

115. THE NATIONAL COUNCIL OF JUVENILE AND FAMILY COURT JUDGES

The National Council of Juvenile and Family Court Judges believes that every family and child should have access to fair, equal, effective, and timely justice. Its mission is to provide all judges, courts, and related agencies involved with juvenile, family, and domestic violence cases with the knowledge and skills to improve the lives of the families and children who seek justice. Founded by a group of judges dedicated to improving the effectiveness of the nation's juvenile courts, NCJFCJ pursues a mission to improve courts and systems practice and raise awareness of the core issues that touch the lives of many of our nation's children and families. The NCJFCJ provides cutting-edge training, wide-ranging technical assistance, and research to help the nation's courts, judges and staff in their important work.

Web site: www.ncjfcj.org

Phone: (775) 784-6012

116.   PRESTON MITCHUM JR. FOUNDATION

The Preston Mitchum, Jr. Foundation is dedicated to addressing the crippling effects of poverty and violence on at-risk youth in our society. They seek to educate, empower and provide a vision of a brighter future for these youth through after-school programming and community-based services.

The Preston Mitchum, Jr. Foundation will accomplish this mission by providing after-school career awareness programs in elementary and middle schools; using the media (television and radio) as both a communication and technical training tool; and sparking the engagement of individuals in the community to give of their time, talent and resources.

Web site: www.pmjfoundation.org

Phone: (410) 529-3844

117. THE URBAN INSTITUTE

The Urban Institute gathers data, conducts research, evaluates programs, offers technical assistance overseas, and educates Americans on social and economic issues in order to foster sound public policy and effective government. Researchers in the Urban Institute's Justice Policy Center produce research, evaluate programs, and analyze data to: help guide federal, state, and local stakeholders in making sound decisions that will increase the safety of communities nationwide; and inform community development to improve social, civic, and economic well-being. Urban Institute researchers examine gender inequalities, racial segregation, and the mutually reinforcing disparities they cause in education, housing, employment, income, and health care.

UI experts analyze race and gender gaps in student test scores, study the persistent discrimination that feeds wealth and income gaps, and explore the unique challenges of single mothers, noncustodial fathers, and hard-to-employ young men—and the public and private programs designed to help them.

Web site: www.urban.org

Phone: (202) 833-7200

118. THE YOUNG PEOPLE'S PROJECT

The Young People's Project develops students aged 8–22 from traditionally marginalized populations into learners, teachers, leaders, and organizers through math and media literacy, community-building, and advocacy in order to build a unique network of young people who are better equipped to navigate life's circumstances, active in their communities, and advocates for education reform in America.

YPP programs create opportunities for high school students to develop through a continuum of experiences across three areas of work: Education, Neighborhoods and Communities, and Education Policy and Advocacy. In each area, training, media, and culture play a critical role in engaging and empowering participants with the tools to see and shape themselves and their communities in new ways.

Web site: www.typp.org

Phone: (617) 354-8991, (617) 354-8994

119. TODD A. BELL NATIONAL RESOURCE CENTER ON THE AFRICAN AMERICAN MALE

The mission of the Todd Anthony Bell National Resource Center on the African American Male is to examine and address critical issues in society that impact the quality of life for African American males throughout their lifespan. The Center plans to achieve these goals by conducting robust research studies and evaluations that inform social policy and theory on African American males and by developing research-based programs, models, and initiatives that could be replicated at other institutions.

Web site: http://odi.osu.edu/current-students/
bell-resource-center/

Phone: (614) 247-4765

120.   U.S. DEPARTMENT OF EDUCATION

The mission of the Department of Education is to promote student achievement and preparation for global competitiveness by fostering educational excellence and ensuring equal access. It houses a database for all government-sponsored, nationwide educational programs, as well as teaching resources for everyday use in the classroom. It engages in four major types of activities: establishing policies related to federal education funding; administering distribution of funds and monitoring their use; collecting data and overseeing research on America's schools; and enforcing federal laws prohibiting discrimination in programs that receive federal funds.

The Department of Education's Early Learning Initiative prioritizes improving the health, social, emotional, and educational outcomes for young children from birth through third grade by enhancing the quality of early learning programs, and increasing the access to high-quality early learning programs, especially for young children at risk for school failure.

Web site: www.ed.gov

Phone: (800) USA-LEARN [(800) 872-5327]

121. UNITED WAY

The United Way believes that the three tenets of education, income, and health are the building blocks for a good life. Working with many partners, United Way continually looks for the most effective ways to help people gain access to educational, economic, and health-related opportunities. In 2008, United Way initiated a 10-year program designed to achieve the following goals by 2018: improving education and cutting the number of high school dropouts—1.2 million students every year—in half; helping people achieve financial stability, and getting 1.9 million working families—half the number of lower-income families who are financially unstable—on the road to economic independence; and promoting healthy lives, increasing by one-third the number of youth and adults who are healthy and who avoid risky behaviors.

Web site: www.unitedway.org

Phone: (703) 836-7112

122. URBAN LEADERSHIP INSTITUTE

ULI prides itself on developing positive youth development approaches designed to provide communities with proactive prevention approaches to reduce delinquency, school failure, substance abuse, and unhealthy decisions among youth. ULI provides a variety of customized Professional Development Workshops for educators, youth counselors, and health educators such as the Center for Male Development (CMD), which addresses many of the challenges that confront male children and youth; and the Dare To Be King Curriculum & Training Program, which is designed to challenge males to confront the never-ending journey of manhood and the responsibility of creating our lives by design, not by default.

Web site: www.urbanyouth.org

Phone: (877) 339-4300 (local) (410) 467-1605

123. URBAN VIDEO GAME ACADEMY (UVGA) WASHINGTON, DC| BALTIMORE| ATLANTA

The Urban Video Game Academy (UVGA) offers after-school and weekend training in the fundamentals of video game design and development. The academy prepares youth for college-level study in video game design and related technology fields such as computer science, digital art, and engineering; enhances learning in academic subjects, such as math and writing; excites and informs youth about career alternatives in the video game design industry, computer science, digital art, and engineering.

Web site: www.uvga.org

Phone: (443) 535-9324

124. VOLUNTEERS OF AMERICA (VOA)

Volunteers of America help the most vulnerable and underserved people achieve their full potential. It provides services that are designed locally to address specific community needs. Common areas of focus include promoting self-sufficiency for the homeless, caring for the elderly and disabled, and supporting positive development for troubled and at-risk children and youth.

VOA's youth programs provide high quality, innovative services for disadvantaged and disconnected children and youth; ensure the social, emotional, and academic development of young children; and empower older youth to be physically, emotionally, and mentally healthy and ready to enter adulthood. Its programs focus on early intervention, delinquency prevention programs, crisis intervention, and long-term services. VOA's family preservation programs help strengthen families by teaching parenting skills and coping techniques, connecting families to a range of services, and providing respite. Its special Operation

Backpack® initiative provides school supplies and backpacks to children in need across the country and helps to fund VOA sponsored after-school and mentoring programs and services for at-risk youth.

Web site: www.voa.org

Phone: (404) 669-0204

125. YMCA

The Y is a cause-driven organization that focuses on nurturing the potential of every child and teen, improving the nation's health and well-being, and giving back and providing support to the neighborhoods they serve. The Y is made up of people of all ages and from every walk of life working side by side to strengthen communities. They believe the values and skills learned early on are vital building blocks for life. At the Y, children and teens learn values and positive behaviors, and can explore their unique talents and interests, helping them realize their potential. Additionally, through leadership and academic enrichment programs such as mentoring, youth and government, and college preparation, the Y makes sure that every child has an opportunity to envision and pursue a positive future, and to take an active role in strengthening his or her community.

Web site: www.ymca.net

Phone: (800) 872-9622

126.   YOUTHFRIENDS

YouthFriends is a nationally recognized and rapidly growing school-based mentoring network involving more than 70 school districts across the states of Missouri and Kansas. YouthFriends connects students, teachers, and schools with inspiring mentors and real-world learning experiences to promote success, encourage healthy behaviors, and build stronger communities. YouthFriends volunteers prove that ordinary people can do extraordinary things. By spending time with students in schools, YouthFriends mentors are making a world of difference in the lives of young people throughout Kansas and Missouri. Volunteers can participate in a wide range of in-school activities, including sharing lunch with a student, reading to a student or class, sharing special talents or career interests, tutoring, or just being a good friend who listens.

Web site: www.youthfriends.org

Phone: (800) 563-0472

127.   YOUTH LEADERSHIP ACADEMY

The Youth Leadership Academy (YLA) is a unique program providing constructive alternatives to gangs, drugs, and other serious problems facing low-income children and their families in high risk neighborhoods. The mission of the YLA is to motivate selected young people from Illinois Community College District 509 who are economically at risk to stay in school, realize their full potential, and become productive leaders and role models in their communities. The goal of the YLA curriculum is to provide cadets with the support and experiences that allow them to reach their full potential as community leaders.

Web site: www.ylaecc.org

Phone: (847) 214-6910

128.   YOUTH SERVICE AMERICA (YSA)

Youth Service America improves communities by increasing the number and the diversity of young people, ages 5–25, serving in substantive roles. YSA supports a global culture of engaged youth committed to a lifetime of service, learning, leadership, and achievement. The impact of YSA's work through service and service-learning is measured in student achievement, workplace readiness, and healthy communities. The YSA's goals are to: educate teachers, community organizations, media, and public officials in the power of youth as problem solvers; and engage children and youth as volunteers, academic achievers, and community leaders.

Web site: www.ysa.org

Phone: (202) 296-2992

129. YOUTH VENTURE

Youth Venture inspires and invests in teams of young people to design and launch their own lasting social ventures, enabling them to have this transformative experience of leading positive social change. Started in the U.S., Youth Venture is now expanding internationally and allows Venturers around the world to connect into a powerful global network. Venturers start businesses, civil society organizations, and informal programs that address all kinds of social issues, including poverty, health, the elderly, the environment, education, diversity issues, and the arts. Youth Venture supports Venturers through the process of designing and launching their ventures, providing guidance, how-to's, and a process for designing and pitching a venture idea.

Web site: www.genv.net

Phone: (404) 669-0204

130. YOUTHBUILD USA

YouthBuild is a highly successful alternative education and community development program that assists youth who are often significantly behind in the basic skills needed to obtain a high school diploma or GED credential. The primary target populations for YouthBuild are adjudicated youth, youth aging out of foster care, and out-of-school youth. Today there are now 273 YouthBuild programs in 45 states; Washington, DC; and the Virgin Islands. Ninety-two thousand YouthBuild students have built 19,000 units of affordable, increasingly green housing since 1994.

YouthBuild USA is dedicated to unleashing the intelligence and positive energy of low-income youth to rebuild their communities and their lives. It believes that every human life is sacred, full of potential, and worthy of love; that young people are capable of playing a leadership role, and if encouraged to do so will bring enormous energy, creativity, and imagination to the work; and that existing leaders should bring young leaders to the table.

Web site: www.youthbuild.org

Phone: (617) 623-9900

RECOMMENDED READING

ACHIEVEMENT GAPS: HOW HISPANIC AND WHITE STUDENTS IN PUBLIC SCHOOLS PERFORM IN MATHEMATICS AND READING ON THE NATIONAL ASSESSMENT OF EDUCATIONAL PROGRESS STATISTICAL ANALYSIS REPORT–JUNE 2011

U.S. Department of Education—NAEP

F. Cadelle Hemphill
Alan Vanneman
NAEP Education Statistics Services Institute
Taslima Rahman
National Center for Education Statistics

http://www.collab4youth.org/Default.aspx
//filename: 2011459.pdf

This report provides detailed information on the size of the achievement gaps between Hispanic and white public school students at the national and state levels and describes how those achievement gaps have changed over time.

http://nces.ed.gov/nationsreportcard/pubs/studies/2011459.asp

AMERICA'S CRADLE TO PRISON PIPELINE: A CHILDREN'S DEFENSE FUND® REPORT

Children's Defense Fund w/ Julia Cass and Connie Curry

http://www.childrensdefense.org/
//filename: cradle-prison-pipeline-report-2007-full-highres.pdf

This report details the massive disparity and inequities within the current educational system that allows disproportionate numbers of minor-

ity youth to fall prey to the preschool-to-prison pipeline.
http://www.childrensdefense.org/programs-campaigns/cradle-to-prison-pipeline/

BUILDING A BRIGHTER FUTURE: AN ESSENTIAL AGENDA FOR AMERICA'S YOUNG PEOPLE

National Collaboration for Youth

http://www.collab4youth.org/Default.aspx
//filename: SchoolSuccessBrief.pdf

School districts and municipalities throughout the U.S. are under intense pressure to reform schools, raise graduation rates, and better prepare American youth for a workforce that must compete globally. This brief cites the importance of a full-range of developmental assets in school, in the home, and in the community that youth need to succeed. It indicates that "meaningful progress in improving educational outcomes must involve multiple stakeholders and a variety of sustained efforts over time."

http://www.collab4youth.org/Resources/Default.aspx

National Human Services Assembly
1319 F Street, NW Suite 402 Washington, DC 20004
Phone: 202-347-2080

FEDERAL SUPPORT FOR ADOLESCENT LITERACY: A SOLID INVESTMENT

Alliance for Excellent Education

http://www.all4ed.org
//filename: FedAdLit.pdf

In March 2007, legislation was introduced in the U.S. House and Senate to authorize the

Striving Readers program, designed to support high-quality reading and writing instruction for millions of students in grades 4–12. But skeptics may wonder: Is there sufficient research to justify a major new federal investment in this area? As this Issue Brief shows, there have been significant findings related to instruction in grades 4–12, the knowledge base on adolescent literacy continues to expand, and the research does indeed provide a solid foundation for effective policymaking.

http://www.all4ed.org/publication_material/
fact_sheets/federal_support_adolescent_literacy_
solid_investment

Alliance for Excellent Education
1201 Connecticut Ave, NW Suite 901
Washington DC, 20036
Phone: 202 828 0828
Fax: 202 828 0821

Man Up: Recruiting & Retaining African American Male Mentors

Urban Leadership Institute
David Miller, M. Ed

http://www.urbanyouth.org/
//filename: 2011459.pdf

This report examines African American male perspectives on mentoring and provides recommendations for grassroots organizations, churches, and governmental entities involved in recruiting & retaining African American males to serve in mentoring programs across the country.

http://www.urbanyouth.org/

MARIAN WRIGHT EDELMAN'S CHILD WATCH® COLUMN

"Promising Models for Reforming Juvenile Justice Systems"

"Bounced Checks From America's Bank of Opportunity"

Marian Wright Edelman

http://www.childrensdefense.org/newsroom/child-watch-columns/

Marian Wright Edelman, President of CDF, speaks to promising models of juvenile justice reform and the promise of "life, liberty, and the pursuit of happiness" through education.

http://www.childrensdefense.org/newsroom/child-watch-columns/child-watch-documents/promising-models-for-reforming.html

http://www.childrensdefense.org/newsroom/child-watch-columns/child-watch-documents/bounced-checks-from-americas-bank-of-opportunity.html

PORTRAIT OF INEQUALITY 2011: BLACK CHILDREN IN AMERICA

Children's Defense Fund

http://www.childrensdefense.org/
//filename: portrait-of-inequality.pdf

This article illustrates the stark difference between racial groups with facts and figures regarding the current status of Black children as compared to other children.

Original Article: http://www.childrensdefense.org/child-research-data-publications/state-of-americas-children-2011/

Recommendations for the Reauthorization of the Elementary and Secondary Education Act Healthy Youth,

National Collaboration for Youth

http://www.collab4youth.org/Default.aspx
//filename: 2010NCY-ESEA_Recommendations.pdf

National Collaboration for Youth offers recommendations for improvements to the reauthorization of the Elementary and Secondary Education Act, commonly known as No Child Left Behind.

http://www.collab4youth.org/Policy/ESEA-NoChildLeftBehind.aspx

Standards and Promising Practices for Schools Educating Boys of Color: A Self-Assessment Tool

The Coalition of Schools Educating Boys of Color (COSEBOC)

http://coseboc.org/index.htm
//filename: COSEBOC_Standards.pdf

A review of relevant scholarly literature leading to the conclusion that there is nothing inherently wrong with boys of color. Rather, the problems are byproducts of social, economic, political, and educational forces that operate within American society and schools.

http://coseboc.org/links.htm
Email: info@coseboc.org
Phone: 855-267-3262

State of America's Children 2011
Children's Defense Fund and Marian Wright Edelman

http://www.childrensdefense.org/
//filename: state-of-americas-2011.pdf

The report illuminates issues which begin in the educational circle and grow to affect the country at large, including health concerns, poverty, gun violence, child welfare, and juvenile justice reform.

http://www.childrensdefense.org/child-research-data-publications/state-of-americas-children-2011/

THE STATE OF BLACK CHILDREN AND FAMILIES: BLACK PERSPECTIVES ON WHAT BLACK CHILDREN FACE & WHAT THE FUTURE HOLDS

Children's Defense Fund and HART Research Associated

http://www.childrensdefense.org/
//filename: The State Of Black Children And Families.pdf (POWERPOINT .PPT)
//filename: the-state-of-black-children.pdf

This PPT is a derivative of the larger study. It details the disconnect between Black adults and children on pertinent social and economic issues and circumstances facing Black Americans.

http://www.childrensdefense.org/child-research-data-publications/data/the-state-of-black-children.html

YES WE CAN, THE SCHOTT 50 STATE REPORT ON PUBLIC EDUCATION AND BLACK MALES

The Schott Foundation for Public Education and Michael Holzman

http://blackboysreport.org/
//filename: bbreport.pdf

This report reveals that there are indeed communities, school districts, and even states doing relatively well in their efforts to enhance opportunities that can raise achievement levels, while others are failing to make the targeted investments necessary to extend what works for Black male students.

http://blackboysreport.org/bbreport.pdf

YOUTH ORGS SHOULD RIDE "SUPERMAN'S" CAPE

Youth Today

Irv Katz

http://www.youthtoday.org/
http://www.dropoutprevention.org/effective-strategies/early-literacy-development

A Blog post revolving around the documentary film: *Waiting for Superman* suggests the country find better ways of attracting top talent and weeding out bad performers in education.

http://www.youthtoday.org/view_blog.cfm?blog_id=414

info@youthtoday.org

Endnotes

Introduction

1. *"Combating the Dropout Epidemic in America,"* Public Media's American Graduate Initiative press release

Chapter One: A Crisis by Any Other Name

2. *Too Important to Fail,* TAVIS SMILEY REPORTS PBS special (Unreleased/ Transcripts courtesy The Smiley Group, Inc. / TS Media)

3. Misani, *"Raising Najee and a generation of Black Boys,"* New York Amsterdam News, Apr 19-Apr 25, 2007, http://findarticles. com/p/news-articles/new-york-amsterdam-news/mi_8153/is_20070419/raising-najee-generation-black-boys/ai_n50659027/

4. Laura Varlas, *"Bridging the Widest Gap: Raising the Achievement of Black Boys,"* ASCD, August 2005, Bridges 4 KIDS, http:// www.bridges4kids.org/articles/2005/8-05/ Varlas8-05.html

5. Stanley L. Johnson, *"Leading Educators Series. An Interview with Dr. Jawanza Kunjufu,"* Journal of African American Males in Education / Leading Educator Series Vol. 2 Issue ½, http:// journalofafricanamericanmales.com/wp-content/uploads/downloads/2011/03/ Jawanza-Kunjufu2.pdf

6. *"Not Prepared for Class: High-Poverty Schools Continue to Have Fewer In-Field Teachers,"* The Education Trust, http://www.edtrust. org/dc/publication/not-prepared-for-class-high-poverty-schools-continue-to-have-fewer-in-field-teachers

7. *"U.S. Education Secretary Arne Duncan to Join Congressman Steny Hoyer and Maryland Lt. Gov. Anthony Brown in Hosting Town Hall Honoring Teachers and Calling on Local Students to Pursue Teaching Career,"* US Department of Education, May 17, 2011, http://www.ed.gov/news/media-advisories/us-education-secretary-arne-duncan-join-congressman-steny-hoyer-and-maryland-0

8. *"CDF Freedom Schools Program,"* Children's Defense Fund: http://www.childrensdefense.org/programs-campaigns/freedom-schools/

9. Kristen Graham, Susan Snyder and Jeff Gammage, *"Arlene Ackerman is out as Philly Superintendent,"* Philly.com / August 22, 2011, Http://www.philly.com/philly/blogs/school_files/arlene-ackerman-is-out-as-philly-superintendent.html

10. Dale Mezzacappa, *"Back to the drawing board: A Promise Academy struggles to move forward,"* The NoteBook / Aug. 25 2011, http://www.thenotebook.org/blog/113991/back-drawing-board-promise-academy-struggles-move-forward

11. Amanda Paulson, *"Study: On average, charter schools do no better than public schools,"* Christian Science Monitor, June 29, 2010, http://www.csmonitor.com/USA/Education/2010/0629/Study-On-average-charter-schools-do-no-better-than-public-schools

12. *"Black Community Crusade for Children,"* Children's Defense Fund, http://www.childrensdefense.org/programs-campaigns/black-community-crusade-for-children-II/

13. *HOME WORKS! The Teacher Home Visit Program*, accessed August 15, 2011 http://www.teacherhomevisit.org/

14. *Alliance for Excellent Education*, August 18, 2011, http://www.all4ed.org/

Chapter Two: Survival Skills: Read or Die

15. *Too Important to Fail,* TAVIS SMILEY REPORTS PBS special (Unreleased/ Transcripts courtesy The Smiley Group, Inc. / TS Media)

16. *"Early Warning! Why Reading by the End of Third Grade Matters,"* The Annie E. Casey Foundation, May 2010, http://www. aecf.org/KnowledgeCenter/Publications. aspx?pubguid={EBC84A89-722A-4985- 9E5D-7AB0803CB178}

17. *"Make Reading by the End of Third Grade a National Priority,"* The Annie E. Casey Foundation, May 18, 2010,http://www.aecf. org/Newsroom/NewsReleases/HTML/2010R eleases/2010KIDSCOUNTSpecialReportRele ased.aspx

18. *"The National Assessment of Educational Progress"* (NAEP), 2010 Report, http://nces. ed.gov/nationsreportcard/

19. *"Early Reading First,"* US Department of Education, http://www2.ed.gov/programs/ earlyreading/index.html

20. *"A Community-Based Model for Saving Children: Geoffrey Canada, President and CEO of the Harlem Children's Zone"* Commencement Speech at Amherst College, 2008, accessed August 20, 2011, https://www.amherst.edu/aboutamherst/ news/specialevents/commencement/ speeches_multimedia/2008/honorands/ canada/node/53642

21. *Urban Prep Academy,* http://www.urbanprep. org/

22. *Urban Prep Academies,* Wikipedia, http://en.wikipedia.org/wiki/Urban_Prep_Academies

Chapter Three: Who's Teaching Black Boys and What Do They Learn?

23. *Too Important to Fail,* TAVIS SMILEY REPORTS PBS special (Unreleased/Transcripts courtesy The Smiley Group, Inc. / TS Media)

24. *"Yes We Can: The 2010 Schott 50 State Report on Black Males in Public Education,"* Shott Foundation, http://schottfoundation.org/publications/schott-2010-black-male-report.pdf

25. Rosa Smith, *"Race, Poverty & Special Education: Apprenticeships for Prison Work,"* The Poverty & Race Research Action Council , November / December 2003, http://www.prrac.org/full_text.php?text_id=938&item_id=8343&newsletter_id=71&header=Education

26. *"A Portrait of Inequality 2011,"* Children's Defense Fund, http://www.childrensdefense.org/child-research-data-publications/data/portrait-of-inequality-2011.html

27. Laura Varlas, *"Bridging the Widest Gap: Raising the Achievement of Black Boys,"* ASCD, August 2005, Bridges 4 KIDS, http://www.bridges4kids.org/articles/2005/8-05/Varlas8-05.html

28. Dr. Ivory A. Toldson, *"Breaking Barriers: Plotting the Path to Academic Success for School-Age African-American Males,"* Congressional Black Caucus Foundation study, 2008, http://www.soros.org/initiatives/usprograms/focus/cbma/articles_publications/publications/breakingbarriers_20080619

29. Tom Burrell, *Brainwashed: Challenging the Myth of Black Inferiority*, (Smiley Books; 1st edition, February 1, 2010)

30. Paul Gorski, *"The Myth of the Culture of Poverty,"* Poverty and Learning Pages 32-36, April 2008 | Volume 65/Number 7, http://www.ascd.org/publications/educational-leadership/apr08/vol65/num07/The-Myth-of-the-Culture-of-Poverty.aspx

Chapter Four: I Don't See Me

31. *Too Important to Fail, TAVIS SMILEY REPORTS* PBS special (Unreleased/ Transcripts courtesy The Smiley Group, Inc. / TS Media)

32. Walter Dean Myers *"Walter Dean Myers: A 'Bad Boy' Makes Good,"* interview with Juan Williams, August 19, 2008, NPR, http://www.npr.org/templates/story/story.php?storyId=93699480

33. *"Meet the Author,"* Walterdeanmyers.com, accessed August 19, 2011, http://www.walterdeanmyers.net/

34. *"Custodial Mothers and Fathers and Their Child Support,"* U.S. Census report, 2007, accessed August 20, 2011, http://www.census.gov/prod/2009pubs/p60-237.pdf

35. David Miller, M.Ed., *"Sober, Responsible Men and Fathers Please Apply,"* Raising Him Alone.com, http://raisinghimalone.com/interviews.htm

36. *"About the Founders: Wade and Cheryl Hudson,"* Just Us Books.com, accessed August 20, 2011,http://justusbooks.com/

37. Cheryl and Wade Hudson, interview by Sylvester Brown, Jr., August 19, 2011

38. Lynda M. Applegate and Susan Saltrick, *"Urban Video Game Academy: Getting in the*

Game," Harvard Business School, January 12, 2007 /N9-807- 122, http://www.hbs. edu/research/publications/2007/cases.html

39. Roderick Woodruff, interview by Sylvester Brown, Jr., August 25, 2011

Chapter Five: Dismantling the Preschool-to-Prison Pipeline

40. *Too Important to Fail,* TAVIS SMILEY REPORTS PBS special (Unreleased/ Transcripts courtesy The Smiley Group, Inc. / TS Media)

41. *"Racial and ethnic fairness/DMC, Reducing racial and ethnic disparities in the juvenile justice system,"* Models for Change.net, http://www.modelsforchange.net/about/ issues-for-change/racial-fairness.html

42. Dr. Jawanza Kunjufu, *"Black Boys and Special Education: Change is Needed,"* Teachers of Color.com, http://www.teachersofcolor. com/2009/04/black-boys-and-special-education-change-is-needed/

43. Geoffrey Canada, "Moving toward manhood," interview with The News Hour with Jim Lehrer, January 20, 1998, http:// www.pbs.org/newshour/gergen/january98/ canada.html

44. Michelle Alexander, *The New Jim Crow: Mass Incarceration in the Age of Colorblindness,* (New Press, The; 1st edition, January 5, 2010)

45. Michelle Alexander, *"Part II: Michelle Alexander on The New Jim Crow: Mass Incarceration in the Age of Colorblindness"* interview with Democracy Now, March 12, 2010, http://www.democracynow. org/2010/3/12/part_ii_michelle_alexander_ on_the

46. Marian Wright Edelman, *"Promising Models for Reforming Juvenile Justice Systems,"* September 4, 2009, Children's Defense Fund, http://www.childrensdefense.org/newsroom/child-watch-columns/child-watch-documents/promising-models-for-reforming.html

47. Dorie Turner, *"Arne Duncan, Spike Lee Urge Black Men To Become Teachers,"* 01/31/11, Huffington Post.com, http://www.huffingtonpost.com/2011/01/31/arne-duncan-spike-lee-black-male-teachers_n_816597.html

48. *5 by 2015 Task Force,* accessed August 26, 2011, 5by2015.org

Chapter Six: Success Psychology for Black Boys: What Will It Take?

49. *Too Important to Fail,* TAVIS SMILEY REPORTS PBS special (Unreleased/Transcripts courtesy The Smiley Group, Inc. / TS Media)

50. Marian Wright Edelman, *"Bounced Checks From America's Bank of Opportunity"*, August 19, 2011, Children's Defense Fund, Child Watch® Column, http://www.childrensdefense.org/newsroom/child-watch-columns/child-watch-documents/bounced-checks-from-americas-bank-of-opportunity.html

51. *"Children are hidden victims of the economic crisis, report says,"* LA Times, August 17, 2011, accessed August 26, 2011, http://latimesblogs.latimes.com/nationnow/2011/08/new-report-spotlights-hidden-victims-of-the-economic-crisis-children-.html

52. *"Disturbing' Report Finds 31 Million U.S. Kids Close to Economic Catastrophe, PBS Report,"*

accessed August 26, 2011, http://video.pbs.org/video/2097206135

53. *"2011 Kids Count Data Book: Promoting Opportunity for the Next Generation,"* Annie E. Casey Foundation report,http://www.aecf.org/~/edia/Pubs/Initiatives/KIDS%20

54. Jerry Shriver, "Vegas' 'bad boy of cuisine' found calling behind bars," 04-03-2011, USA TODAY, http://www.usatoday.com/printedition/life/20070223/dd_prisonchef23.art.htm

55. Jeff Henderson, interview by Sylvester Brown, Jr., August 21, 2011

56. Staff, "Bev Smith, Dr. Boyce Watkins Join Town Hall on State of the Black Male," June 16, 2011, Black World.com, http://yourblackworld.com/2011/06/16/bev-smith-dr-boyce-watkins-join-town-hall-on-state-of-the-black-male/

57. "Black Perspectives on What Black Children Face and What the Future Holds," January 2011, Children's Defense Fund, http://www.childrensdefense.org/programs-campaigns/black-community-crusade-for-children-II/bccc-assets/the-state-of-black-children.pdf

58. Dr. Ivory A. Toldson, "Breaking Barriers: Plotting the Path to Academic Success for School-Age African-American Males, 2008" / Congressional Black Caucus Foundation, http://www.soros.org/initiatives/usprograms/focus/cbma/articles_publications/publications/breakingbarriers_20080619

59. CDF Freedom Schools, Children's Defense Fund, accessed August 27, 2011, http://www.childrensdefense.org/programs-campaigns/freedom-schools/

60. "23rd Annual 100 Black Men of America Conference Draws Record Numbers," Today's Drum.com, accessed August 24, 2011, http://todaysdrum.com/6043/23rd-annual-100-black-men-of-america-conference-draws-record-numbers-raises-funds-for-education-outreach-programs/

61. Laura Varlas, "Bridging the Widest Gap: Raising the Achievement of Black Boys," ASCD, August 2005, Bridges 4 KIDS, http://www.bridges4kids.org/articles/2005/8-05/Varlas8-05.html

62. Langston Hughes, "Let America be America Again," poem (Originally published in Esquire 1938), accessed August 25, 2011, http://www.mindfully.org/Reform/Hughes-America-Again1938.htm

Acknowledgments

It takes a village to raise a child and in this case it's taken several villages at The Smiley Group to bring *Too Important to Fail,* the documentary, to viewers, and T*oo Important to Fail: Saving America's Boys,* the book, to readers.

To the West Coast village of TAVIS SMILEY REPORTS in Los Angeles, I offer a standing ovation to my extraordinary team including executive producer Coby Atlas, producer Sasheen Artis, supervising producer Pat Bischetti, our brilliant editor Judy Lieber, and our production coordinator Maleena Lawrence, who shared my vision and passion for this project. And of course we couldn't have ever produced such an inspiring piece of work without the contributions of Allan Palmer, Darryl Smith, Sam Sewell, Susumu Tokunow, Andre Artis, Sid Lubitsch, Boryana Alexandrova, Marcus Bleeker, and Mike Kelly.

To the East Coast village of SmileyBooks in New York, I extend my deep gratitude and awe of the hard work and the dedication it took to complete this book in such record time. A special thanks to SmileyBooks president and project editor Cheryl Woodruff, writer extraordinaire Sylvester Brown, designer Juan Roberts for our extraordinary cover, and SB staffers Kirsten Melvey and Thomas Louie for helping to "make it happen."

To PR magician Leshelle Sargent who worked this project wearing two hats—getting the word out for both TAVIS SMILEY REPORTS and SmileyBooks—please accept our coast to coast thanks.

A very special thank you to Denise Pines and Carolyn Fowler who made invaluable contributions to this project and kept the train on the track behind the scenes.

I would also like to acknowledge Dr. Alfred Tatum for his generous and invaluable expert reading of the text.

Last and hardly least, my sincere thanks to Patricia Harrison, president and CEO of the Corporation for Public Broadcasting, and CPB itself for their generous funding of the television special and for their wisdom in launching the American Graduate: Let's Make It Happen initiative to end America's dropout crisis.

About
TAVIS SMILEY
REPORTS

TAVIS SMILEY REPORTS, a series of primetime specials, debuted in January 2010 with "One on One with Hillary Clinton." The next, "MLK: A Call to Conscience," aired on March 31, and the series continued when Smiley teamed up with Academy Award–winning director Jonathan Demme to commemorate the fifth anniversary of Hurricane Katrina in "New Orleans: Been in the Storm too Long" on July 21. The fourth episode premiered December 29 with an inside look into music programs for schools and a one-on-one conversation with L.A. Philharmonic's music director, Gustavo Dudamel.

Too Important to Fail is part of American Graduate: Let's Make It Happen, a public media initiative supported by the Corporation for Public Broadcasting to help local communities across America find solutions to address the dropout crisis. For web-exclusive content, visit www.too importanttofail.com.

TAVIS SMILEY REPORTS is produced for PBS by The Smiley Group, Inc./TS Media, Inc.

Executive producer is Jacoba Atlas. Funding is provided by The California Endowment, W.K. Kellogg Foundation, and the National Education Association (NEA).

About Tavis Smiley

Tavis Smiley is host of the nightly talk show *Tavis Smiley* on PBS, and host of *The Tavis Smiley Show* and co-host of *Smiley & West* from Public Radio International (PRI). Smiley launched America I AM: The African American Imprint, a world-class traveling exhibition celebrating the extraordinary impact of African American contributions to our nation and the world. The exhibit is on a four-year, ten-city tour and is currently on display in St. Louis, Missouri. Smiley is also the author/editor of 15 books, including *The New York Times* bestsellers *Covenant with Black America* and *What I Know for Sure: My Story of Growing Up in America*. His most recent book is *FAIL UP: 20 Lessons on Building Success from Failure*. In 2009, *TIME* magazine named him one of the World's Most Influential People.

For more information, visit www.tavistalks.com.

SmileyBooks Titles of Related Interest

BOOKS

FAIL UP:
20 Lessons on Building Success from Failure
by Tavis Smiley

THE COVENANT In Action
Compiled by Tavis Smiley

AMERICA I AM LEGENDS:
Rare Moments and Inspiring Words
Edited by SmileyBooks
Introduction by Tavis Smiley

AMERICA I AM BLACK FACTS:
The Timelines of African American History
1601-2008
By Quintard Taylor

NEVER MIND SUCCESS...GO FOR
GREATNESS!
The Best Advice I've Ever Received
by Tavis Smiley

HOPE ON A TIGHTROPE:
Words & Wisdom
by Cornel West

PEACE FROM BROKEN PIECES:
How To Get Through What
You're Going Through
by Iyanla Vanzant

BLACK BUSINESS SECRETS:
500 Tips, Strategies and Resources for
African American Entrepreneurs
by Dante Lee

BRAINWASHED:
Challenging the Myth of Black Inferiority
by Tom Burrell

DVDs/CDs

STAND: a film by Tavis Smiley

All of the above are available at your local
bookstore, or may be ordered online through
Hay House (see contact information on next page)

We hoped you enjoyed this SmileyBooks publication.
If you would like to receive additional information, please contact:

SMILEYBOOKS

www.smileybooks.com

Distributed by:
Hay House, Inc.
P.O. Box 5100
Carlsbad, CA 92018-5100
(760) 431-7695 or (800) 654-5126
(760) 431-6948 (fax) or (800) 650-5115 (fax)
www.hayhouse.com® • www.hayfoundation.org

Published and distributed in Australia by: Hay House Australia
Pty. Ltd. • 18/36 Ralph St. • Alexandria NSW 2015 • *Phone:* 612-
9669-4299 • *Fax:* 612-9669-4144 • www.hayhouse.com.au

Published and distributed in the United Kingdom by: Hay House
UK, Ltd. • 292B Kensal Rd., London W10 5BE • *Phone:* 44-20-8962-
1230 • *Fax:* 44-20-8962-1239 • www.hayhouse.co.uk

Published and distributed in the Republic of South Africa by: Hay
House SA (Pty), Ltd. • P.O. Box 990, Witkoppen 2068 • *Phone/Fax:*
27-11-467-8904 • www.hayhouse.co.za

Published and distributed in India by: Hay House Publishers India
• Muskaan Complex, Plot No. 3, B-2, Vasant Kunj, New Delhi 110
070 • *Phone:* 91-11-4176-1620 • *Fax:* 91-11-4176-1630 • www.
hayhouse.co.in

Distributed in Canada by: Raincoast • 9050 Shaughnessy St.,
Vancouver, B.C. V6P 6E5 • *Phone:* (604) 323-7100 • *Fax:* (604) 323-
2600 • www.raincoast.com

CPSIA information can be obtained at www.ICGtesting.com
Printed in the USA
LVOW091504050312

271672LV00001B/118/P